Business Cycles

B

BUSINESS CYCLES

Theory and Evidence

Andy Mullineux, David G. Dickinson and WenSheng Peng

BLACKWELL
Oxford UK & Cambridge USA

Copyright © Andy Mullineux, David G. Dickinson and WenSheng Peng 1993

The rights of Andy Mullineux, David G. Dickinson and WenSheng Peng to be identified as authors of this work have been asserted in accordance with the Copyright, Designs and Patents Act 1988.

First published 1993

Blackwell Publishers
108 Cowley Road
Oxford   OX4 1JF
UK

238 Main Street, Suite 501
Cambridge, Massachusetts 02142
USA

British Library Cataloguing in Publication Data
A CIP catalogue record for this book is available from the British Library.

Library of Congress Cataloging-in-Publication Data
Mullineux, A. W.
    Business cycles : theory and evidence / Andy Mullineux, David G.
Dickinson and WenSheng Peng.
        p.   cm.
    Includes bibliographical references and index.
    ISBN 0–631–18566–6 (alk. paper). – ISBN 0–631–18567–4 (pbk.)
    1. Business cycles. I. Dickinson, David G. II. Peng, WenSheng,
Dr.   III. Title.
    HB3711.M82   1993
    338.5′42–dc20   92–26627   CIP

ISBN 0–631–18566–6
       0–631–18567–4 Pbk.

Typeset in 11 on 13pt Times
by Graphicraft Typesetters Ltd., Hong Kong

This book is printed on acid-free paper

To our Parents and Partners

Contents

List of figures   ix

List of tables   x

Preface   xii

1 Introduction   1

2 Equilibrium Business Cycles: Theory and Evidence   5

    2.1 Introduction   5
    2.2 Early Contributions and the Basic Model   5
    2.3 Extensions to the Basic Model   9
    2.4 Empirical Evidence   15
    2.5 Summary   23

3 Non-linear Business Cycle Modelling   25

    3.1 Introduction   25
    3.2 Cycles in Linear and Non-linear Models   28
    3.3 Non-linear Business Cycle Modelling   34
    3.4 Empirical Evidence of Chaos and Non-linearity   53
    3.5 Summary   61

4 Political Business Cycles, Reputation and Credibility   64

    4.1 Introduction   64
    4.2 The Electoral Economic Cycle   66

4.3   Game Theory, Reputation, Credibility and   67
      Optimal Monetary Policy Design
4.4   Partisan Cycles   74
4.5   Empirical Evidence Relating to the 'Political   77
      Business Cycle'
4.6   Summary   83

5   **Empirical Evidence Relating to Business Cycles:**
    New UK Results in Context   85

5.1   Introduction   85
5.2   Non-stationarity and Shock Persistence in UK   85
      Macroeconomic Variables
5.3   A VAR Model of the UK Business Cycle   92
5.4   Evidence of Political Business Cycles in the UK   100
5.5   Chaos, Non-linearity and Macroeconomic   109
      Variables
5.6   Summary   118

6   **Evaluation and Conclusions**   120

6.1   Introduction   120
6.2   An Overall Evaluation   120
6.3   Policy Implications   122
6.4   Suggestions for Future Research   123

Bibliography   131

Index   156

List of figures

3.1	Solution paths to the linear deterministic multiplier–accelerator model.	30
3.2	Sensitivity to initial conditions.	34
3.3	The stages of Kaldor's cycle.	37
3.4	Rose's non-linear Phillips curve.	40
4.1	The dynamic inconsistency of zero inflation.	70
4.2	Reputation acquisition and policy choice.	72
5.1	Responses to a one standard deviation demand shock.	99
5.2	Responses to a one standard deviation labour supply or productivity shock.	100
5.3	Responses to a one standard deviation cost or supply shock.	101
5.4	Responses to a one standard deviation money shock.	102
5.5	Responses to a one standard deviation real exchange rate shock.	103
5.6	Phase portraits I.	111
5.7	Phase portraits II.	112
5.8	Phase portraits III.	113
5.9	GP plots I.	114
5.10	GP plots II.	115

List of tables

5.1	Unit roots test results, 1956:I–1991:III	90
5.2	Estimates of the persistence measure $A(1)$	91
5.3	Cointegration test results, 1956:I–1991:III	92
5.4	Unit roots test results, 1963:I–1991:III	96
5.5	Variance decomposition of RGDP	97
5.6	Variance decomposition of UNEMR	97
5.7	Variance decomposition of GDPP	97
5.8	Variance decomposition of M_4	97
5.9	Variance decomposition of REX	98
5.10	Regression on real GDP growth, dependent variable y_t; 1960:I–1991:III	104
5.11	Regression on unemployment rate, dependent variable U_t; 1960:I–1991:III	105
5.12	Regression on inflation rate, dependent variable π_t; 1960:I–1991:III	106
5.13	Regression on money growth, dependent variable M_4; 1963:I–1991:III	107
5.14	Regression on money growth, dependent variable M_4; 1963:I–1991:III	107
5.15	Regression on fiscal surplus/deficits, dependent variable z_t; 1961:I–1991:III	108
5.16	Regression on fiscal surplus/deficits, dependent variable z_t; 1961:I–1991:III	109
5.17	BDS statistics, real GDP; 1956:I–1991:III	116
5.18	BDS statistics, nominal GDP; 1956:I–1991:III	116
5.19	BDS statistics, unemployment rate; 1959:I–1991:III	117
5.20	BDS statistics, real consumption; 1956:I–1991:III	117

5.21 BDS statistics, real capital formation;
1956:I–1991:III 117
5.22 BDS statistics, consumer price index;
1956:I–1991:III 118

Preface

This book is a development of the lectures given by David Dickinson and Andy Mullineux to students on the undergraduate and postgraduate economics and money, banking and finance (MBF) programmes offered by the Department of Economics at the University of Birmingham (UK). With the generous assistance of the Principal Research Fund of the School of Social Science, they were fortunate to be able to employ WenSheng Peng as a Research Associate to assist with the project.

Chapters 2 and 3 of the book are shortened and simplified versions of survey articles published in the *Journal of Economic Surveys*, 1992–3 (see Bibliography). Chapter 2, written by David Dickinson and Andy Mullineux, covers equilibrium business cycles; and chapter 3, written by Andy Mullineux and WenSheng Peng, covers non-linear business cycle modelling. Chapter 4, on political business cycles, credibility and reputation, expands on the lecture notes of David Dickinson and Andy Mullineux. These three chapters develop significantly previous work by Andy Mullineux (1984, 1990) relating to these topics. Chapter 5, which is largely the work of WenSheng Peng, investigates the business cycle properties of UK macroeconomic time series by testing for unit roots, non-linearity and political influences, *inter alia*, and compares the results with those obtained in previous studies of UK and US macroeconomic data. The concluding chapter summarizes the empirical evidence, draws policy conclusions and provides suggestions for furture research.

As a whole, the book aims to provide a critical survey of business cycle research, and to compare the results of empirical studies pertaining to the business cycle in the US and the UK with a view to suggesting avenues for future research. Because empirical research into business cycles in the UK has been much less extensive than in the US in recent years, it was necessary to derive some new results for the UK. These are presented in chapter 5.

The book is intended for use by (third year) undergraduate and postgraduate students of macroeconomics and monetary theory and policy, and professional economists wishing to keep abreast of developments in this important, but all too often neglected, area of economics.

Andy Mullineux
David Dickinson
WenSheng Peng

Department of Economics
University of Birmingham
June 1992

1

Introduction

Interest in business or trade cycle theory is itself cyclical. In periods of sustained prosperity interest wanes, as it did in the 1960s and early 1970s, when research into macroeconomic dynamics concentrated on growth theory. At the end of the 1960s the continued existence of business cycles was even questioned (Bronfenbrenner, 1969). However, the experiences of the mid- and late 1970s and early 1980s brought about a resurgence of interest in business cycles. For the purposes of this book we shall take a very broad view of the meaning of the term 'business cycle', namely: the existence of (negative) serial correlation in key real macroeconomic aggregate series, such as output and unemployment, and nominal series, such as inflation, and comovements between various series; in the sense that there are leading or lagging (as well as coincident) relationships between them over time, which may or may not imply causality.

Mullineux (1984, ch. 3) traces the renewed interest of academic economists in business cycle theory to the contributions of Nordhaus (1975), who revived interest in the political business cycle (PBC), and Lucas (1975), who utilized rational expectations to revitalize interest in the equilibrium business cycle (EBC). Nordhaus's approach differed from previous PBC literature (Kalecki, 1943; Boddy and Crotty, 1975) in stressing the influence of the electoral period, rather than class conflict, on the cycle in economic activity and drew on ideas being developed by 'modern political economists' (Tullock, 1976; Frey, 1978; Tufte, 1978) who used the work of Downs (1957) and argued that governments manipulate the economy to maximize their share of votes cast in elections (see also Mullineux, 1984, section 3.3; Alt and Chrystal, 1983). Lucas (1975) regarded Hayek (1933) as an antecedent of his work. Lucas's monetary EBC (MBC) model marked a major departure from the Keynesian approach to business cycle modelling, which regarded the cycle as an essentially disequilibrium phenomena. In Keynesian models 'rigidities' or 'frictions' in the economy, such as sticky nominal wages and prices, are the proximate cause of disequilibrium, and cycles are generated using mechanisms such as multiplier – accelerator interaction (Haberler, 1946; Hansen, 1957). The 'modern' equilibrium approach to business cycles, associated with Lucas and other members of the 'New Classical School' (Sargent and Wallace, 1975, 1976; Barro, 1976), aimed to derive the dynamic stochastic behaviour of the macroeconomy from the basic microeconomic principles of rational, maximizing firms and households and, in so doing, to make use of advances in microeconomic theory relating to the intertemporal supply of labour. Lucas (1977) provides an informal discussion of the theory.

The EBC approach evolved from highlighting the role of unanticipated monetary shocks in driving fluctuations, to one which emphasized the importance of real shocks. The real business cycle (RBC) literature is reviewed in chapter 2. In contrast, after a burst of academic interest in the late 1970s and early 1980s, the interest of the economics profession in the PBC was sustained largely by journalistic economic commentary, although there has been a resurgence of work in this area in the late 1980s. This will be discussed in chapter 4. Like the PBC approach, Lucas's MBC approach received little attention at the National Bureau of Economic Research (NBER) Conference in the mid-1980s and was rejected in Gordon's overview of the conference (Gordon, 1986, p. 9), for reasons that are discussed in chapter 2.

One might have expected adherents of the 'New Classical School' to view the economy as being essentially stable, but displaying erratic movements by virtue of being hit by a series of random shocks, as postulated by the 'Monte Carlo' hypothesis. Many eminent economists and statisticians, including Irving Fisher, have disputed the very existence of business cycles. Fisher (1925) argued that business cycles could not be predicted because they resembled cycles observed by gamblers in an honest casino. The periodicity, rhythm or pattern of the past, to the extent that it really exists, is of no help in predicting the future. Mullineux (1990, section 1.2) reviews evidence concerning the Monte Carlo hypothesis). Alternatively, the Slutsky (1937) approach of viewing the cycle as the result of summing (filtering) random causes (real and monetary shocks) might have been adopted (see Lines, 1990). However, Lucas (1975) utilized a modified version of the acceleration principle, much favoured in Keynesian cycle models (Samuelson, 1939), to explain the persistence of the effects of the shocks and a number of 'stylised facts' distilled from the extensive statistical analysis of economic data by the NBER. The mechanics of Lucas's acceleration process were supply led, rather than demand led as in a Keynesian framework. Barro (1981, ch. 2) provides further details on the MBC approach and also presents a survey of alternative approaches to explaining 'persistence'.

Although an equilibrium theory of the cycle, in the sense that all markets are assumed to clear continuously, the Lucas (1975) model remained in the Frisch (1933) tradition that had dominated Keynesian econometric model building in the late 1960s and early 1970s. As a result, the cycle was not endogenously determined by the economic model. Instead, it was driven by temporary external random shocks, the energy from which was transformed into a cycle (around a growth trend) by an essentially linear propagation model which provided a mechanism for the effects of the shocks to persist over time. Mullineux (1990, section 1.4) and Lines (1990) provide further discussion of the Frisch–Slutsky hypotheses. In MBC models, temporary shocks enter via a random error term and unanticipated changes in the growth of the money supply. The monetary shocks must be temporary by virtue of the rational expectations hypothesis (REH). Mullineux (1984, section 3.2) provides further discussion.

Despite the widespread rejection of the MBC models, largely because of their reliance on unrealistic informational deficiencies (Okun, 1980; Gordon, 1986), the EBC approach itself was not abandoned. In its place real EBC (RBC) models proliferated in the 1980s. These models also followed the Frisch (1933) approach by developing alternative linear propagation and shock-generating models. They retained the rational expectations hypothesis (REH) but postulated that real, as opposed to monetary, shocks were the major source of impulses. While emphasizing technological shocks in particular, the RBC models of the early and mid-1980s, like the MBC models before them, focused on key intertemporal relationships. Towards the end of the 1980s, the RBC approach was broadened to make use of dynamic recursive techniques to solve agent optimization problems subject to market clearing conditions, in a general model of economic growth.

In the next chapter, the theoretical literature on the EBC, and particularly the RBC, approaches to business cycle modelling is reviewed and the empirical evidence supporting this approach is appraised. It is concluded that this approach has made a valuable contribution to our understanding of business cycles, but cannot fully explain the phenomenon. The following two chapters explore alternative explanations of business cycles which emphasize the role of non-linearities (chapter 3) and political factors (chapter 4). Again, the emphasis is on recent theoretical contributions and the empirical evidence supporting these approaches is appraised. A key difference between many of the models and approaches reviewed in chapters 3 and 4 and the EBC approach is that the latter relies on shocks to drive the equilibrium cycle, while the former can generate cycles endogenously (and often in equilibrium) in the absence of shocks, which merely add to realism by providing an additional source of irregularity (and uncertainty).

In chapter 5 an empirical analysis of UK macroeconomic aggregate time series is undertaken, in order to test a number of basic hypotheses relating to business cycle modelling. No attempt is made to derive and test a particular business cycle model. The linearity hypothesis underlying the EBC approach is tested, for example, and tests are also made for political influences on key macroeconomic aggregates, such as output, inflation and unemployment, and policy instruments. The results of the time series analysis are then assessed in the context of previous findings, using alternative methods and data sets, for the UK and the US.

The concluding chapter provides an overall assessment of the level of understanding of the business cycle phenomena in the light of the review of the literature and the empirical evidence. Some policy implications are drawn and suggestions are made for future research.

2

Equilibrium Business Cycles: Theory and Evidence

2.1 Introduction

This chapter surveys equilibrium business cycle (EBC) theory, which has dominated the business cycle literature since the mid-1970s. It focuses primarily on the real business cycle (RBC) literature, which has the monetary equilibrium business cycle (MBC) model developed by Lucas (1975) as its antecedent. RBC and MBC models are themselves related to a wider class of linear stochastic business cycle models which, following Frisch (1933), view the cycle (around the growth trend) as the result of the propagation, by the economic system, of a series of random shocks. The MBC approach highlighted the importance of monetary shocks, but its failure to adequately explain observed fluctuations provided the impetus to the development of the RBC approach, which emphasizes the importance of real shocks. This chapter also appraises the empirical support for the RBC approach, and finds it less than compelling. Given the failure of Keynesian, and equilibrium linear stochastic business cycle models fully to explain economic fluctuations, the Frischian approach to business cycle modelling is called into question. Developments to existing EBC models, which may help to clarify our understanding of business cycle behaviour, are also discussed and the chapter concludes with an assessment of the progress made with EBC models.

2.2 Early Contributions and the Basic Model

While retaining the EBC approach and the REH, RBC models assume that information is publicly and costlessly available. The 'signal extraction problem' that is a key ingredient of the MBC models is thus discarded, and consequently unanticipated monetary shocks are of no importance. The rejection of the MBC model meant that the RBC theorists had to look to the real economy for both disturbances and the propagation mechanism. The most influential early contributions to the RBC literature were those of Kydland and Prescott (1982) and Long and Plosser (1983).

The basic hypothesis of RBC models, that economic cycles are the Pareto optimal outcome of agent's optimizing reactions to real (supply and demand) shocks, is conceptually straightforward, but the resulting models are technically difficult to solve. Individuals are assumed to optimize intertemporally by choosing labour input and, given the budget constraint, current consumption and wealth (capital stock). As there are shocks to the real economy, individuals will need to revise their optimal plans and consequently there will be an impact on output, consumption and employment trends. By distinguishing between temporary and permanent shocks, and through the introduction of other features such as production lags (Kydland and Prescott) or a complex input–output structure (Long and Plosser), it is possible to generate a very rich set of dynamic possibilities. Whether these are sufficient to model the actual behaviour of economies is something we turn to later.

Formally, RBC models start with maximization by individuals of the present value of current and future utility which, in a temporally additively separable form, can be written as:

$$U_t = \sum_{s=t}^{\infty} U_s(C_s, L_s) (1 + \theta)^{(t-s)}, \qquad (2.1)$$

where C_s is the consumption at time s, L_s is the labour supplied at time s, $U(..)$ is a single-period utility function (which could be time dependent) and θ is the discount rate. Economic agents substitute consumption from one period to the next via capital accumulation. Hence there is a per period budget constraint:

$$C_s + K_{s+1} = w_s L_s + K_s, \qquad (2.2)$$

where K_s is the capital stock inherited at time s and w_s is the wage rate set at time s in a competitive labour market.

In order to close the model it is necessary to specify the production technology, and it is from this that the RBC model developed. We can assume that output is a function of inputs:

$$Y_s = F(K_s, L_s, \xi_s) \tag{2.3}$$

with, as shown above, a productivity shock ξ_s. This is one particular way of introducing the real shock which will generate the type of cyclical response required. It is not, of course, the only way. It is assumed that $E(\xi_s) = 0$. This, then, is the basic model. The goods and factor markets are assumed to be perfect and the dynamic path of the economy can be solved from the agents' optimization problem described in equations (2.1)–(2.3), with market clearing imposed. When assumptions are made about the form of individual preferences, and the technology used, the solution (which may be closed-form or a linear approximation) can be shown to be

$$C_s = C(K_s, \{\xi_s\}), \ L_s = L(K_s, \{\xi_s\}), \ K_{s+1} = K(K_s, \{\xi_s\}), \tag{2.4--6}$$

where ξ_s is the set of all future productivity disturbances. If these are known then equations (2.4), (2.5) and (2.6) map out the perfect foresight equilibrium. However, if they are not known then it is assumed that economic agents use all available information to form expectations of the time path of the $\{\xi_s\}$, in which case the solution is a rational expectations equilibrium. The form of the dynamic paths followed are dependent upon the key technological and preference relationships. For example, the more persistent the effects of shocks are, the longer lasting will the output effects be. Similarly, the lower the rate of time preference which economic agents have, the more influence a shock now will have into the future. If intertemporal substitution is high, then we would expect to see significant shifts in the amount of labour supplied as a result of productivity disturbances.

Long and Plosser (1983) adopted a highly restrictive formulation, of the class of model described above, assuming the following: rational expectations; complete current information; no long lived commodities; no frictions or adjustment costs; no government; no money; and no serial correlation in the shocks. Their aim was to focus on the explanatory power of fundamental neoclassical hypotheses about intertemporal consumer preferences and the production process. The preference function employed implies that the representative consumers will spread unanticipated increases in wealth over both time and consumer goods, including leisure. There is, therefore, persistence in the effects of changes in wealth, since they alter the demand for goods over time. The production possibility hypothesis also allows for a wide range of intra- and intertemporal substitution possibilities by adopting a sectoral approach to production. In emphasizing intertemporal substitution, their analysis is consistent with the MBC approach (see Lucas (1977) in particular). As in Black (1982), the business cycle equilibrium is preferred to non-business cycle alternatives, and agents are willing to take risks to achieve higher expected returns. Random shocks are added to the outputs of numerous commodities, which are used for consumption or as inputs into the production process. Input–output relationships propagate the effects of output shocks both forward in time and across sectors but, unlike Black's model, there are no adjustment costs and so unemployment is difficult to explain.

Zarnowitz (1985, p. 567) acknowledges the importance of sectoral changes in tastes and technology as a cause of numerous shifts in relative prices and outputs, and that these changes may have an impact on growth, but does not believe that they can explain recurrent sequences of expansions and contractions in aggregate activity, i.e. business cycles. Nevertheless, Long and Plosser's work usefully highlights the potential role of input–output relationships. It is, therefore, richer than the Kydland and Prescott (1982) single-product model, and moves away from the 'islands' hypothesis inherent in MBC models, which effectively denies any multiplier process. Long and Plosser use stochastic simulations with random shocks to test whether their propagation model can produce a realistic cyclical output. The propagation mechanism is found to display damped cyclical responses to shocks. Therefore, it can generate cycles, in the Frischian tradition, if hit by a series of shocks of suitable frequency and size. Furthermore, comovements in industrial outputs can potentially be identified as a result of input–output relationships.

Kydland and Prescott (1982) modify the neoclassical equilibrium growth model (Solow, 1970) by introducing stochastic elements and an alternative 'time to build' technology, in place of the constant returns to scale neoclassical production function. In so doing they reject the adjustment cost technology often emphasized in empirical studies of aggregate investment behaviour. Their approach is, therefore, to integrate neoclassical growth theory and business cycle theory. The preference function chosen assumes a relationship between the current value and the past history of leisure. This allows a great deal of intertemporal substitution of leisure, in line with MBC models. This feature does not increase persistence in their model but does change agents' reaction to it. The persistence of the effects of shocks is instead the result of the 'time of build' assumption, that multiple periods are required to build new capital goods and only finished capital goods are part of the productive capital stock.

The technology parameter is subject to a stochastic process with two components, permanent and temporary, akin to Friedman (1957). Productivity itself cannot be observed, but an indicator of it can be observed at the beginning of the period. Consequently, a 'signal extraction problem' is present, but it is different from the Lucasian one. The permanent component is highly persistent, and shocks are therefore autocorrelated. When the technology parameter grows smoothly, steady state growth prevails; but when it is stochastic, cyclical growth results.

2.3 Extensions to the Basic Model

The Kydland and Prescott and Long and Plosser analyses stimulated a vast amount of academic work on the causes of economic cycles. This research programme continues, but has at its centre the idea that if cycles exist they must be explained as the rational reaction of economic agents to economic events. Additionally, within the market clearing paradigm considerable progress has been made in integrating growth theory into an equilibrium business cycle framework. Such models generalize the very specific approaches of the early work in this area.

King et al. (1988a) present a neoclassical growth model augmented by choice of labour supply as the basic framework for their RBC analysis. Growth is the result of capital accumulation, which is driven by an exogenously specified rate of labour-augmenting technical change. Fluctuations around the growth trend are caused by productivity or technology shocks, and the normal intertemporal substitution of consumption and labour which drives the growth model. As in previous work, including Kydland and Prescott (1982), the non-linear first order conditions derived from the Lagrangian are linearized, using an approximation method, prior to analysing the dynamic behaviour of the model and its empirical implications.

In a natural extension to their analysis, King et al. (1988b) explore the effects of modifying the basic neoclassical growth model in line with Romer (1986) and Lucas (1988), whose modifications to the neoclassical growth model permit the long-run growth rate to be the endogenous outcome of a time invariant technology (see also Stadler, 1990). King et al. introduce constant returns to scale Cobb–Douglas production functions in an extended model with two capital stocks, physical capital and human capital. Commodity output depends on whether resources are allocated to the production of final goods, including physical capital, or to the production of human capital. Different temporary technology shocks affect each of the production functions and have permanent effects on the level of economic activity, because they permit temporary changes in the amount of resources allocated to growth. The endogenous growth model, therefore, generates integrated time series, the first differences of which are stationary and invertible, even when the underlying shocks are stationary. King et al. believe that these properties of the model originate from the underlying constant returns to scale structure needed to generate endogenous steady state growth.

Analysing a variant of the endogenous growth model, King et al. (1988b) show that shocks to either of the production processes affect the time profile of both capital stocks, and have permanent effects on levels of variables such as output and consumption. Because of the permanent effects of the shocks, the endogenous growth models enhance the propagation mechanism of the basic neoclassical model. They do not attempt to test whether series generated by such models resemble observed macroeconomic time series, but they do suggest that this approach to RBC modelling offers a promising avenue for future research, a conclusion with which it is easy to agree.

In response to the theoretical and empirical failure of the MBC models, the RBC approach attributes much less significance to the influence of money on the economy. King and Plosser (1984) introduce money as a factor of production by viewing it as a way of reducing the costs of transactions which are incurred during production as a result of frictions caused, perhaps, by informational deficiencies. Money and credit levels are determined endogenously within an optimizing framework but, as such, the model can only explain the cyclical pattern of nominal variables as an endogenous response to developments in the real economy. There is no possibility of exogenous monetary influences exerting any effects on the real economy.

Williamson (1987) introduces financial intermediation, justified by the existence of asymmetric information and monitoring costs, into an EBC model. As a result, a credit supply mechanism, which gives rise to rationing, acts in tandem with intertemporal substitution to propagate stochastic disturbances. The amount of credit rationing varies over the cycle, and the model is related to the New Keynesian literature (Stiglitz and Weiss, 1981; Scheinkman and Weiss, 1986). The model mimics observed qualitative comovements when subject to real disturbances, but there are several inconsistencies with empirical evidence when it is subject to monetary disturbances. The model therefore provides support for the RBC approach and casts doubt on the MBC approach. Bencivenga and Smith (1991) introduce financial intermediation into a model of endogenous growth and demonstrate that the provision of liquidity services will promote economic growth. Their paper highlights further the need to incorporate the financial sector into RBC models.

Eichenbaum and Singleton (1986) note that, with the exception of King and Plosser, little consideration had been given to the extent to which RBC models emerge as special cases of monetary models of the business cycle. Like Lucas (1987), they conclude that acceptance or rejection of RBC models must be based in part on the plausibility of the variances and autocorrelations of technology shocks employed to generate realistic cycles.

Kydland and Prescott (1982), for example, simply chose variances and levels of persistence of shocks that were consistent with those of observed variables, and concentrated on the adequacy of the model for propagating the time profiles of key aggregate economic indicators comparable to US data. To explore the extent to which RBC models emerge as special cases of EBC models, Eichenbaum and Singleton derive an EBC model for a monetary economy in which monetary growth can have real effects. A 'cash-in-advance' constraint (Lucas and Stokey, 1984) is the only source of non-neutrality in the model; which is an extended version of Garber and King (1983) and is closely related to the Long and Plosser (1983) model. They examine the conditions under which the RBC special case, in which the cash-in-advance constraint is not binding, provides an accurate approximation to the monetary economy. They find a constant monetary growth rate to be both necessary and sufficient for the real allocations to be identical in the MBC and RBC versions. There is clear evidence, however, that monetary growth has not been constant. This alone is not sufficient to dismiss the RBC explanation of aggregate fluctuations, since the cash-in-advance constraint may be incorrectly imposed. They also show that when real shocks to tastes and technology predominate, the RBC will be a good approximation to the MBC model with constant monetary growth.

Commenting on Eichenbaum and Singleton (1986), Barro (1986) emphasizes their warning that the lack of significance of monetary shocks as a determinant of output does not imply that RBC models are correct. For example, Keynes's (1936) model is clearly not an RBC model. It attributes a major role to endogenous shocks, in the form of shifts in optimism and pessimism (or animals spirits) of investors (see also Azariardis, 1981), and the propagation mechanism relies on wage–price rigidities.

Lucas (1987) also suggests a synthesis of RBC with MBC models, in which monetary shocks play an important role. He demonstrates that money can be grafted on to the Kydland and Prescott (1982) model in a way that has no significant effect on its conclusions. However, he does not believe money to be neutral in the short run, and argues that the fluctuations observed in the real world are too large to be induced by a combination of real impulses and Kydland and Prescott's propagation mechanism. He draws attention to the work of Friedman and Schwartz (1963, 1982), which clearly implies an influence of money on economic activity and concludes that either larger, including monetary, shocks are required, or that the propagation model must be modified to include larger multipliers.

Lucas (1987) speculates about how a hybrid model, with preferences and technology for producing goods akin to those postulated by Kydland and Prescott (1982), but without centralized trading, would behave. Instead of the centralized trading assumed by Kydland and Prescott, he postulates the Lucas and Stokey (1984) motivation for using money. Agents are assumed to trade in securities at the beginning of the period, and to use the cash acquired in the course of this trading to buy consumer goods later in the period. Lucas then postulates that the money supply is erratic, following a stochastic process with parameters fixed and known by agents, and considers the conditions under which monetary expansion will be associated with real expansions. One possibility would be to retain the full public information assumption, utilized by Kydland and Prescott and by Lucas and Stokey, but to introduce price rigidity, perhaps using wage contracts in the manner of Taylor (1979).

Lucas's preferred method of introducing monetary effects is to integrate MBC models with RBC models (see also Froyen and Waud, 1988; Cooley and Hansen, 1989). He notes that in a multiproduct version of the Kydland and Prescott (1982) model, the volume of necessary information would explode, if the full public information assumption were retained. If there is a cost of processing information, then economic agents will economize and process only the information which substantially sharpens their ability to make production or investment decisions. As a result, the 'signal extraction problem' is reinstated, and a positive supply response to monetary shocks can be expected. Lucas believes that, in a modified version of the Kydland and Prescott (1982) model, elaborated to admit limited information due to costs of processing it, shocks of a monetary origin would be 'misperceived' by agents as signalling a change in technology or preferences. Monetary shocks would then trigger dynamic responses that are similar to the technology shocks considered by Kydland and Prescott. He notes that Lucas (1975) had relied on 'misperceptions' over whether the shocks were real or nominal in origin, but had not specified the source of the real shocks, which had been introduced simply through random error terms. Lucas cites Grossman and Weiss (1982), Grossman et al. (1983) and other models, surveyed in Scheinkman (1984), as examples of models employing limited information and allowing for an interplay of real and monetary shocks.

Lucas (1987) also draws attention to the Sargent (1976) paper, which demonstrated the 'observational equivalence' of models in which monetary non-neutrality is the result of limited information and those in which money affects real variables in some other way. Lucas concludes his analysis by advocating the use of: (1) a structural model that lays down specific economic hypotheses for testing, rather than the employment of reduced form testing; and (2) a dynamic game-theoretic analysis (the game being played between policy-makers and economic agents), in the light of the 'Lucas critique' (see Lucas, 1976).

The initial work on RBC models concentrated on closed-economy versions. This resulted largely from their application to the relatively closed US economy. There have been some recent attempts to incorporate open-economy aspects into this class of model. Cantor and Mark (1988) and Stockman (1990) consider aspects of open-economy RBC models. Cantor and Mark focus attention on the international transmission of RBCs, driven by country-specific real technology shocks, through international securities markets. Stockman also considers the dynamics of international transmission, and derives implications of RBC models for variables, such as the balance of trade and terms of trade, which do not appear in closed-economy RBC models.

Mendoza (1991) investigates whether an open-economy RBC model is consistent with two well identified empirical regularities found in many economies. These are that domestic saving and investment are positively correlated and, secondly, that the current account and balance of trade move countercyclically (see Backus and Kehoe, 1989). The crucial element added to the standard RBC model is that trade in foreign financial assets can be used to finance trade imbalances. This also plays a role in explaining domestic saving and investment correlations.

Mendoza uses a conventional type of RBC model which effectively incorporates a terms of trade shock within the standard productivity shock. In addition, he incorporates a real interest rate disturbance that can be interpreted as a world shock. The model can provide simulations once calibration of the model has taken place. Because of the ability to finance trade imbalances with financial assets, the presence of adjustment costs allows investment to be controlled without a corresponding effect on consumption, and hence he achieves a much better fit with actual behaviour than in a closed-economy model. However, the simulations provide results that are inconsistent with the real world in terms of exaggerating, among other things, the behaviour of consumption over the cycle. The reason for this is that the real rate of interest is exogenous in the model. Overall, however, the model provides encouraging results, and further work on the open-economy aspects of RBC models is clearly appropriate (see also Backus et al. (1990) and Schlagenhauf and Wrase (1991) as examples of very recent work).

Other extensions to the RBC approach consider variations on the one or more key assumptions of the model. Smith (1989a,b) has analysed the effect of introducing heterogeneous agents. This introduces the possibility of unemployment in equilibrium and of magnifying the effects of shocks on hours worked, if agents have private information about their own productive abilities. Greenwood et al. (1988) consider the idea of variable utilization of capital. An effect of this is to provide a channel for investment shocks to impinge on labour market equilibrium and hence reduce the reliance on intertemporal substitution to propagate shocks. The role of inventories, often claimed to be a key source of cyclical fluctuations (see Blinder and Maccini, 1991), has been developed beyond the very limited way in which they were introduced by Kydland and Prescott (1982). For example, Haltiwanger and Maccini (1988) consider them as alternatives to lay offs when firms are uncertain about demand, while Cooper and Haltiwanger (1990) investigate their use as a source of intertemporal redistribution, hence adding to the dynamic possibilities of equilibrium models. Finally, work is also starting on the key role that fiscal policy can play in affecting equilibrium. Barro (1989) provides a survey of fiscal policy affects in standard growth models. King et al. (1988b) consider how an output tax used to finance government expenditure and transfer payments generates a sub-optimal equilibrium. Dotsey (1990), Barro (1990) and Greenwood and Huffman (1991) include further developments. This is likely to be a growing area of interest for EBC theorists.

2.4 Empirical Evidence

In our review of the theoretical development of the RBC model, we emphasized that it grew out of dissatisfaction – both theoretically and empirically – with early work which incorporated rational expectations into an equilibrium framework. The empirical analysis of the Friedman/Phelps/Lucas price-misperceptions model was initially supportive (Lucas, 1972; Barro, 1977; Attfield et al., 1981), but later work, allied to its basic theoretical implausibility, led to its demise (Barro and Hercowitz, 1980; Gordon, 1982; Mishkin, 1982; Merrick, 1983).

Some later work has provided support for the surprise supply function. Kretzmer (1989), for example, considers the relationship between unexpected monetary changes and industry specific output, and finds evidence that this disaggregated approach is supportive of the basic Lucas hypothesis. Meanwhile, Chan (1988) argues that earlier work, with some exceptions (such as Kormendi and Meguire, 1984), had not paid enough attention to the impact of regime changes, and presents evidence in favour of the contention that, when proper account is taken of them, the monetary misperceptions approach has some empirical validity. However, this new evidence has not led as yet to a re-evaluation of the earlier rejection of the basic Lucas hypothesis, but does provide evidence of the need to incorporate monetary factors into an equilibrium framework.

Kydland and Prescott (1982) analysed the empirical relevance of their version of the RBC model using calibration and simulation. The reason for adopting this solution technique was that the programming problem they used to explain the decision of the representative agent was too complicated to allow a tractable analytic solution to be found. The approach taken by Kydland and Prescott was to use well established empirical results to assign values to calibrate the behavioural parameters of the decision problem they investigated. These included the coefficient of relative risk aversion and the rate of capital depreciation. They then evaluated the time paths of the key macroeconomic variables for particular values of the productivity shocks, which drive the whole model. They compared the simulated economy with the stylized facts of the US economy (see Zarnowitz (1985), Greenwald and Stiglitz (1988) and Blackburn and Ravn (1990, 1991) for detailed discussions of the stylized facts).

The way in which Kydland and Prescott set up the productivity shock structure is crucial to giving them enough degrees of freedom to achieve a reasonable match between simulated and actual behaviour. As discussed in section 2.2, there are two components to the productivity innovation – permanent and temporary. In addition, the observation of productivity is assumed to be contaminated with noise and hence there is a signal extraction problem. This structure allows considerable flexibility in generating different simulations of the dynamic behaviour of the aggregate economy using the RBC model. Even with this flexibility, Kydland and Prescott need to assume that the productivity shock is highly persistent, with a first order autocorrelation coefficient close to one. The implication that productivity follows a (near) random walk is an issue to which we return later.

The model does achieve a respectable correlation with certain key real world statistics. For example, while the predicted absolute variations (around trend) of consumption and investment are not consistent with the actual values, the model does pick out the fact that the variability of consumption is less than that of output, while that of investment is greater. Also, the contemporaneous correlations between output and consumption, and investment and capital stock derived from the Kydland and Prescott model are close to those observed in practice. Their results proved to be sensitive to the specification of the investment technology, and the 'time to build' lag is important, but the cycle is not particularly sensitive to the length of the lag. Experimentation with adjustment costs, as an alternative source of persistence, proved unfruitful, which tends to refute the multisectoral analysis of Black (1982). However, Kydland and Prescott express the view that the introduction of heterogeneity in the capital stock should prove a worthwhile modification of their basic model.

Kydland and Prescott (1988) introduce variable utilization of the capital stock and find that, as a result, a smaller productivity shock is required to mimic real world behaviour. This is important, since the original Kydland and Prescott specification has been criticized for requiring productivity shocks to be too large. Alternatively, the source of shocks can be extended beyond productivity. For example, Mendoza's (1991) open-economy model includes a terms of trade shock.

As has been discussed, the RBC model can be nested within the standard neoclassical growth model. King et al. (1988a) have found that an RBC model, based securely within this paradigm, can provide simulations which are consistent with certain important aspects of the actual behaviour of the aggregate economy. In particular, when only temporary shocks are included, the model fails to generate serial correlation in output and employment consistent with the real world, but when productivity behaves very much like a random walk the results are more consistent with the data. This is a very similar observation to that for the Kydland and Prescott model. It should also be noted that, rather than filtering the data to render it stationary, King et al. include, in their baseline specification, a deterministic growth model to explain the trend. As we shall discuss later, there is evidence to suggest that whether or not data is filtered can have a significant effect on empirical analysis. King and Rebelo (1989) point out that the neoclassical (Solow) model of economic growth does not explain cross-country differences well. This point is taken up by Mankiw et al. (1990) who argue that, generally, the model performs well, and that the key to understanding cross-country differences is to introduce endogenous growth through human-capital accumulation.

However, there are a number of empirical shortcomings with the real business cycle approach, and it is important to take them into account when evaluating it. First, the fact that the cycle is driven mainly by productivity disturbances has been the subject of extensive debate (see, for example, McCallum, 1986). Solow (1957) decomposed growth in output into growth resulting from increasing the input of factors of production and a residual, which he defined as growth in factor productivity. Despite Solow's conclusion that the residual explains the major part of growth, and Prescott's (1986) estimation that its variability is large enough to generate the required dynamics, many economists have expressed the view that it is too constricting an interpretation. For example, the Solow approach is widely regarded as over-estimating the size of the productivity shock (e.g., see McCallum, 1989). Interpreting oil-price shocks in terms of productivity does help but, as Barro (1986) points out, these are still not large or frequent enough to provide the necessary sequence of shocks. Indeed, Barro sees the problem as one of multipliers, and the lack of them in RBC models. Eichenbaum (1991) argues that real business cycle models should not be relied upon, since small variations in model specification generate large differences in the character of the results.

A second area of concern for RBC theorists is the inability adequately to explain labour market behaviour. The failure to replicate the significant variability in hours worked is perhaps not surprising in that an optimizing, market clearing, model explains unemployment as an extended vacation. Kydland and Prescott introduced greater intertemporal substitution of labour by making the marginal utility of leisure dependent on past values, but they were still unable to explain the large variation in numbers of workers employed.

A number of extensions of the basic model have been introduced in order to provide a better explanation of labour market behaviour. Hansen (1985) introduced an indivisible labour supply (and hence corner solutions) as a way of rationalizing the identification of labour supply variability with changes in the number of people working. This has also proved to be a fruitful method of analysing micro data (see, e.g., Rogerson and Rupert, 1991). Kydland (1984) used the idea of heterogeneity in the labour market. Introducing different reservation wages in the presence of heterogeneity can lead to large changes in employment for relatively small changes in wages. The use of the multisectoral model of Long and Plosser with costly job changes can also add richness to labour market dynamics (Lillien, 1982; Rogerson, 1987) and there is clearly a role for formal search theory within a real business cycle model. Note, however, that the observation that job vacancies and unemployment do not move together (Abraham and Katz, 1986) is inconsistent with the basic search model (although Davis (1987) generates results consistent with cyclical behaviour of employment by carefully specifying the time of reallocation across sectors). While these equilibrium approaches are important innovations, the conclusion should be that the labour market appears to be so imbued with rigidities (e.g., implicit/explicit contracts, unions and labour hoarding) that attention must be paid to these before a full explanation of behaviour can be claimed. Such rigidities lie at the heart of the new Keynesian counterattack to the equilibrium approach (see Greenwald and Stiglitz, 1988).

A third area of concern for the empirical evaluation of real business cycle models is the lack of a role for monetary factors, which have always been seen to be crucial to explaining the short-run behaviour of the aggregate economy. Some empirical support for ignoring money has been found (Sims, 1980, 1982; Litterman and Weiss, 1985). Sims (1980, 1982) finds that money plays a significant role in explaining output as long as nominal (short-run) interest rates are not included in the model. However, as McCallum (1983) points out, the monetary authorities were using the interest rate as the policy instrument during the period of investigation. Litterman and Weiss (1985) focus on the behaviour of the real interest rate and demonstrate that it is not (Granger-) caused by output, money, prices or nominal interest rates. Since the real interest rate is the key transmission mechanism for monetary policy in conventional macroeconomic models, this is not only supportive of models which ignore money, but damaging to the conventional analysis. Eichenbaum and Singleton (1986) point out that the Litterman and Weiss test is sensitive to whether log levels or differences are used, and demonstrate that only differenced variables produce the neutrality result. Christiano and Ljungquist (1988) argue that the power of the first difference result is low and favour using levels. Further work by Stock and Watson (1988) and Krol and Ohonian (1990) confirmed these results. Although more work is clearly required in this area, the evidence appears to favour assigning money at least some role in causing output variation, although perhaps not through conventional macroeconomic models (see also Boschen and Mills (1988) and Bernanke (1986) for support of this proposition).

The sources and sizes of shocks, the behaviour of the labour market and the influence of money have been three key areas in which the original simulations of the real business cycle models have been found to be deficient. However, other methods have been employed to evaluate the real business cycle approach empirically. Since we shall use such methods for our own empirical work, they will now be reviewed.

The analysis of money and its effects on the economy, which was discussed above, generally used vector autoregressions (VARs) and variance decompositions. This methodology has been employed more generally to evaluate the importance of real shocks in explaining output variation. Such work ranges from Blanchard and Watson (1986), demonstrating that cycles are not all alike and consequently casting doubt on the efficacy of the stylized facts approach, to the Shapiro and Watson (1988) and Blanchard (1989) attempts to decompose the sources of fluctuations in output. Shapiro and Watson find that aggregate demand shocks account for most of the variation in hours worked, while technological shocks are significant short-run determinants of output change. Blanchard finds that demand shocks are dominant in the short run, while supply shocks explain the bulk of long-run variability. Norrbin and Schlagenhauf (1988) use the DYMIMIC (Engle and Watson, 1981) approach to decompose output into aggregate, regional and industry-specific shocks. This allows an informal test of the importance of the multisector model of Long and Plosser and, since they define output fluctuations as employment fluctuations, of the sectoral approach to explaining labour markets. They find support for giving importance to aggregate and industry-specific shocks, but limited effects of regional shocks. Chrystal and Dowd (1989) disaggregate UK output data into industry specific form, and find little support for the view that demand policy variables have any impact.

The second way in which evidence supporting the RBC approach has been presented is through analysis of the dynamic time series properties of key macroeconomic aggregates. This work was initiated by Nelson and Plosser (1982), who were interested in whether key macroeconomic aggregates exhibited unit roots (i.e. were random walks). If they could be modelled as stochastic trends rather than as mean-reverting (cycles about a deterministic trend), this would be supportive of the real business cycle approach (although other approaches such as chaos (Brock and Sayers, 1988) or conventional macroeconomic models (Durlauf, 1989) could equally well generate this result).

Nelson and Plosser (1982) used the Dickey–Fuller test (see, for example, Dolado et al., 1990) and found that of all the macroeconomic variables (including output, real wages and consumer prices, for example) considered, only in the case of unemployment could the null hypothesis of a unit root be rejected. Schwert (1987) points out that it is likely that aggregate variables will have significant moving average components, and that the presence of these will reduce the power of the Dickey–Fuller tests. Perron and Phillips (1987) use a test procedure which takes account of this by providing estimates of the 'nuisance parameters' emanating from the moving average specification. These are used to provide a transformation of the conventional Dickey–Fuller statistics and the proposition that GNP does have a unit root is tested. They find that, while they are able to reject a unit root for pre-World War II data, they are unable to reject it for the postwar period. However, as is discussed by Perron and Phillips and expanded upon by Clarke (1989), Schwert (1989) and Kim and Schmidt (1990), the tests have low power in small samples. This point is also taken up, in a general context, by Cochrane (1991).

Clarke's paper extends the analysis to a range of different countries and finds that the data are generally consistent with the trend/mean reversion concept. A new test, proposed by Hylleberg et al. (1990), incorporates seasonal factors into the unit root test. Evidence from Otto and Wirjanto (1990) suggests that it may be important to include seasonal dummies. The results of unit root tests have also been criticized on the grounds that they do not take into account the difference between large infrequent and small frequent permanent shocks. Perron (1989) argues that if explicit account is taken of the 1973 oil-price shock then the postwar series of GNP does not contain a unit root. Balke and Fomby (1991) take the analysis further, and argue that the large infrequent and small frequent shock hypotheses are observationally equivalent. For the UK, Mills and Taylor (1989) and Walton (1988) find evidence in favour of a unit root in output.

Another approach to the issue of the statistical persistence of aggregate shocks can be found in Campbell and Mankiw (1987, 1989). They argue that if output fluctuations are temporary, then an unexpected change in output should not affect forecasts of output in the future. In their earlier paper, they test this proposition for US data. Their later work extends it to a number of different economies. By estimating output as an ARIMA process, Campbell and Mankiw demonstrate that there is a considerable degree of persistence in the response of output to shocks, a result also discussed by Watson (1986). They also use a nonparametric approach due to Cochrane (1988) which concurs with their result. It should be noted that the only economy which is not consistent with the persistence hypothesis is that of the UK (although recent work by Mills (1991b) is supportive for post-World War II output). Furthermore, the results are sensitive to the use of the ARIMA specification. In addition, Watson (1986) uses an unobserved components model, in which the persistence is found to be considerably less.

Malliaris and Urrutia (1990) utilize the variance ratio test suggested in Cochrane (1988) to re-examine the claims of Nelson and Plosser (1982). They find that the random walk component is significant but that, specifically, the variability of the unemployment rate, real wages, real GNP *per capita* and industrial production contain important temporary components.

Finally, consideration of unit roots leads naturally into the concept of cointegration (for a recent survey, see Dolado et al., 1990). Little work has been done on macroeconomic time series, but a recent paper by Kunst and Neusser (1990) has investigated the cointegrating properties of selected Austrian aggregate variables. They find that the behaviour of the Austrian economy is not consistent with the basic properties of the RBC model. King et al. (1991) also use the concept of cointegration, and argue that productivity shocks explain less than half the variation in output, but that incorporating nominal variables does not add further explanatory power.

2.5 Summary

This chapter has analysed the theoretical and empirical aspects of the equilibrium approach to modelling business cycles. In so doing, it has highlighted a number of key features:

- The real business cycle model has developed out of dissatisfaction with the theoretical underpinning and empirical shortcomings of the Lucas monetary misperceptions approach.
- In utilizing an equilibrium framework, it has relied upon the intertemporal substitution which lay at the foundation of the MBC model.
- It has eschewed any monetary factors and relied exclusively on real shocks to generate movements in the aggregate economy.
- While certain key features of short-run economic behaviour (and, in the context of growth models, long-run behaviour) have been adequately explained, there has been an unfortunate reliance on implausibly large productivity shocks.
- In addition, the failure to incorporate monetary factors and the (related) inability to explain labour market behaviour are

seen as major obstacles to widespread acceptance of this model as the only explanation of macroeconomic behaviour.

However, there are sufficient grounds for examining the applicability of the theory to the UK and, in chapter 5, we shall utilize the two main empirical approaches which have been introduced, namely VARs and unit root tests. These will provide some indication of whether or not it is worthwhile going on to build an RBC model of the UK economy.

3

Non-linear Business Cycle Modelling

3.1 Introduction

As noted in chapter 2, the real business cycle (RBC) approach to business cycle modelling provided the dominant paradigm in the 1980s. In line with the postwar tradition, the cycle is modelled using essentially linear or log-linear relationships to transform (propagate) the energy provided by external or exogenous random or autocorrelated shocks into a cycle, in the manner suggested by Frisch (1933). It differs from the traditional Keynesian approach in that the propagation model is firmly based on neoclassical microeconomic foundations, and throughout the cycle the economy is continuously in equilibrium. A major impact of the RBC approach has been to require adherents to competing paradigms to provide rigorous microeconomic underpinnings to their macroeconomic theories, as the the New Keynesians have done (Greenwald and Stiglitz, 1987).

As the 1980s progressed, momentum gathered behind a radically different approach to modelling economic fluctuations based on the relatively new mathematical theory of chaos. Chaos theory demonstrates that remarkably simple non-linear systems can yield incredibly complex dynamic paths involving cycles of various periods and seemingly random series. Furthermore, the actual path followed is highly sensitive to the starting value. Because the theory of chaos is still relatively new, the dynamic possibilities have only been rigorously analysed for relatively few systems, which are small by the standards of economic modelling. Larger and more complex systems have, however, been analysed using computer simulations and do not seem to indicate markedly increased complexity in behaviour. However, they do suggest that, in more complex non-linear systems, chaotic behaviour and cycles of various periods become more likely (Boldrin and Woodford, 1990).

Deterministic non-linear models are, therefore, capable of producing output that is seemingly random or which displays complex cyclical behaviour; in the sense that the cycles produced appear to have no regular period and, unlike sine or cosine waves, are asymmetric. The addition of multiplicative or additive random error terms to such models, rendering them stochastic, seemingly increases the likelihood of complex dynamics and therefore, irregularity (Samuelson, 1947; Kelsey, 1988). Hence they provide an alternative to the traditional linear stochastic (Frischian) approach to business cycle modelling.

The non-linear business cycle models developed in the 1980s have not yet progressed to the stage at which they can be subjected to rigorous econometric testing. In contrast, the Kydland and Prescott (1982) RBC model has been estimated, but only after imposing 'reasonable' (based on extraneous empirical studies) values on certain parameters. As noted in section 2.4, the results to date have not been conclusive. The RBC models have normally been assessed by their ability to explain selected 'stylized' facts, such as comovements between various economic time series identified by the National Bureau of Economic Research (NBER). Significantly, the reason why it is difficult to test RBC models directly is that they are often non-linear, and non-linear econometric testing procedures are not well developed. Consequently, the empirical assessment is normally based on linearized versions of the models. The same difficulty confronts economists wishing to test deterministic non-linear cycle models. They cannot contemplate linearization, however, because it would eliminate the complex dynamic behaviour (George, 1981; George and Oxley, 1991).

Having opted for linear stochastic modelling procedures, economists naturally concentrated on developing linear econometric testing procedures. This was convenient, since it enabled well developed statistical and mathematical techniques to be adapted to economic analysis and empirical testing relatively easily. The potential pitfalls of blind adherence to the linearity assumption were illustrated by Blatt (1978) and Frank and Stengos (1988a). In both papers, output is generated by a non-linear model;

in Blatt's case a modified version of the famous Hicks (1950) trade cycle model discussed in section 3.3. The simulated model's output is then examined using standard econometric tests and found to be consistent with the Frischian hypothesis – that it is generated by a linear stochastic model – which, of course, it is not! This raised the possibility that the profession had prematurely rejected non-linear cycle modelling: either due to laziness, because linear modelling is more tractable; or because of inadequate econometric testing. Blatt's critique (see also Blatt, 1980; Mullineux, 1990, ch. 1) appeared prior to the recent explosion of interest in non-linear equilibrium models, so the 'premature rejection' relates to earlier non-linear business cycle modelling associated with Keynesians such as Hicks, Kaldor and Goodwin. Their approach differed from the non-linear equilibrium modelling in that the latter emphasizes the fact that economic equilibrium is maintained throughout the cycle, which has a well developed behaviourial foundation, as in the RBC literature. In contrast, the older Keynesian non-linear models concentrated on macroeconomic behaviour, did not develop microeconomic foundations, and often emphasized disequilibrium behaviour. 'Keynesian', 'chaos' and other non-linear cycle models are surveyed in section 3.3.

Given that statistical and econometric techniques are not yet sufficiently well developed to allow RBC and non-linear business cycle models to be tested directly, alternative procedures for assessing the relevance of the non-linear approach are needed. In principle, it is possible to test whether a series is chaotic or random. To obtain reliable results, however, large data sets are required, possibly numbering tens of thousands (Chen, 1988; Ramsey et al., 1990). This is an extremely tall order in economics, where laboratory experimentation and trials cannot be used to generate results. It is possible, however, to test for the presence of non-linearities (although the tests do not yet reveal the nature of the non-linearities) with much shorter series. Because non-linearity is a necessary (though not sufficient) condition for chaos, this is clearly important, and evidence of the presence of strong non-linearity in macroeconomic data would pose a serious challenge to the (log-)linear approach to macroeconomic modelling. Such issues are discussed in section 3.4.

A common feature of many of the RBC models, as emphasized in King et al. (1988a,b), is the attempt to explain both growth and

the cycle using a modified neoclassical growth model. The cycles
are typically driven by persistent technological shocks. The generation of the shocks, and the reasons for their persistence, are
not adequately explained, as discussed in chapter 2. Non-linear
equilibrium models share with RBC models an emphasis on
equilibrium behaviour and fluctuating growth. Both approaches,
therefore, focus on dynamic development and economic evolution.
We use the term 'dynamic economic development' to avoid confusion with 'evolutionary economics', which rejects the neoclassical approach. Evolutionary economists look to Marx, Keynes
and Schumpeter *inter alia* for inspiration. Schumpeter's work, for
example, attempted to explain why economic development progressed along a cyclical growth path, and treated innovations or
technical change as endogenous, rather than exogenous as in the
RBC models. Shackle (1968) also attempted to explain dynamic
economic development and attributed a major role to innovations
but, like Schumpeter (1934, 1935, 1939), did not formulate a
mathematical model. Unfortunately, we have not space in which
to discuss these theories in this book (see section 4 of Mullineux
and Peng (1992) and Ford and Peng (1993) for further discussion). In the next section, the qualitative features of linear and
non-linear deterministic and stochastic models are illustrated.

3.2 Cycles in Linear and Non-linear Models

Samuelson (1939) clearly demonstrated the dynamic paths that
can be derived from a simple linear version of the traditional
'multiplier–accelerator' model, which collapses to a second order
difference equation in national income with two parameters, the
multiplier and the accelerator. The basic Samuelson model is as
follows:

$$Y_t = g_t + C_t + I_t, \tag{3.1}$$
$$I_t = b(C_t - C_{t-1}), \qquad C_t = aY_{t-1}, \tag{3.2, 3.3}$$

where Y_t is national income, g_t is government expenditure, C_t is
consumption expenditure, and I_t is induced private investment.
Substituting equations (3.2) and (3.3) into (3.1), and assuming
that g_t is constant over time, the following second order, linear,
non-homogeneous difference equation is obtained:

$$Y_t - a(1 + b)Y_{t-1} + abY_{t-2} = g. \tag{3.4}$$

The equilibrium value of Y_t (the particular solution) is:

$$Y^* = g/(1 - a). \tag{3.5}$$

The complete solution is:

$$Y_t = A_1\lambda_1^t + A_2\lambda_2^t + Y^*, \tag{3.6}$$

where the roots of the characteristic equation, λ_1 and λ_2, are

$$\lambda_{1,2} = \tfrac{1}{2}\{a(1 + b) \pm \sqrt{[a(1 + b)]^2 - 4ab}\}. \tag{3.7}$$

The actual dynamic path of Y_t depends on the relationship between the parameters (which in turn determine the roots of the characteristic equation). Broadly, following an initial disturbance from equilibrium and according to the parameter values, five outcomes are possible: non-oscillatory convergence ($a \leq 1, b < 1$); oscillatory convergence ($1/a > b$); oscillatory divergence ($1/a < b$); non-oscillatory divergence ($a \leq 1, b > 1$); and persistent oscillation of constant amplitude and period (which turn out to be conservation oscillations – see below) ($1/a = b$). These different time paths are illustrated in figure 3.1, as cases A–E respectively.

Qualitatively, these are the only options available with deterministic (non-stochastic) linear difference equations (even if the order of the equation is increased). Dynamic paths emanating from differential equations are qualitatively similar (although the parameter relationships or conditions on values of the roots of the characteristic equation required to generate them are different), except that the dynamic paths are continuous and do not display the discrete jumps or 'steps' that typify the dynamic paths of the solutions to deterministic difference equations.

Most economists accept the need to use stochastic models, although they do not often make it clear why this is so. Among the most obvious sources of shocks are the influences of variables omitted from the model: either due to lack of knowledge; or because of the need, again due to data constraints, to limit the size of the model (see section 6.4 for further discussion). In addition, many variables are regarded as exogenous, i.e. determined outside the model. They may be variables that are themselves subject, at least at times, to shocks or chaotic behaviour, e.g. the weather. In projecting forward, for predictive purposes, their

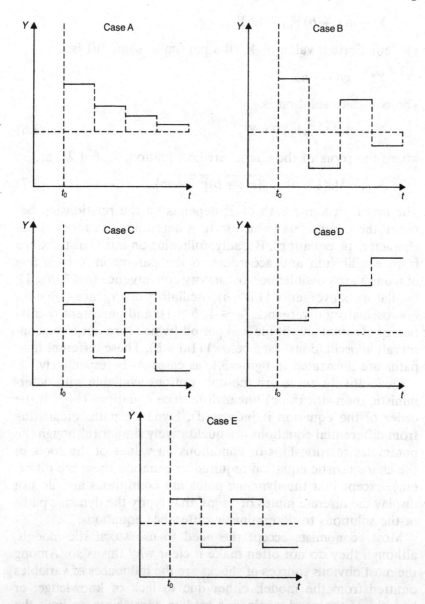

Figure 3.1 Solution paths to the linear deterministic multiplier–accelerator model.

values are typically extrapolated (often using relatively sophisticated, albeit linear, techniques) from past behaviour. Deviations from their extrapolated paths are likely to occur in practice and random error terms (typically additive) are included (rendering the model stochastic) to allow for this.

The presence of random shocks alters the qualitative features of the linear deterministic model significantly. In the case of the Samuelson multiplier–accelerator model outlined above, the conservative cycle option (case E) might appear to be the most promising one for explaining the cycle. However, it is one of the least likely outcomes, since it requires the accelerator to be the reciprocal of the marginal propensity to consume. Most of the other dynamic paths could arise over quite wide parameter ranges and so have a higher probability of occurring. Conservative cycles are so named because they conserve all energy, and the random shocks inherent in a stochastic model can be regarded as providing energy. Over time, following repeated shocks, the conservative cycle would therefore increase in amplitude, as demonstrated by Klein and Preston (1969), who used a discrete version of the Dresche model discussed in Samuelson's *Foundations* (Samuelson, 1947). This case then becomes indistinguishable from oscillatory divergence (case C) in linear stochastic models.

Thus, to model the business cycle using linear stochastic systems, various options are possible. In the damped oscillatory case, new energy is required, in the form of repeated shocks, to offset the dampening (normally attributed to friction in mechanics). This is the approach advocated in Frisch (1933), and which has formed the basis of most postwar business modelling. In the nonoscillatory convergence case, fluctuations are still possible if the system is subjected to repeated shocks which input something resembling an oscillation. In this case the propagation (economic) model imparts little persistence and the cycle is driven by the shocks (Slutsky, 1937). In practice, RBC models represent something of a hybrid of these two approaches. Like the proceeding large-scale Keynesian econometric models (Adelman, 1960; Hickman, 1972), the RBC models do not impart enough persistence to propagate temporary random shocks into output resembling economic time series (see section 2.4 for further discussion). When the shock-generating mechanism is modified to produce autocorrelated (or 'persistent') shocks, however, the output from the propagation model is more realistic. Thus the energy source itself contributes some of the serial correlation in the output series.

However, these are not the only possibilities for generating cycles, but in order to exploit the others the linearity assumption must be abandoned. Hicks (1950), whose model is discussed in more detail below, introduced a ceiling and a floor on investment and a ceiling on output. Explosive tendencies are accordingly contained and, provided that the economy does not crawl along the floor or the ceiling (Mathews, 1959), economic fluctuations will occur as the economy, prone as it is to oscillatory or non-oscillatory divergence, bounces between ceiling and floor and thus oscillates around a growth trend. In his *Foundations*, Samuelson (1947) labelled this type of non-linearity a 'billiard table non-linearity'. This is because abrupt, discontinuous, changes of direction or qualitative behaviour occur at certain points (e.g. when the ball hits the cushion). Such (type I) non-linearity models differ from type II non-linear models, which contain functions that, although non-linear, are continuous and hence have no discontinuities. Despite the absence of discontinuities in type II models, abrupt changes in qualitative behaviour can still occur at certain parameter values or points. Points at which abrupt changes of behaviour occur are commonly called 'bifurcation points' (or 'bifurcations') in the mathematics literature. Bifurcations are solely features of non-linear models. In section 3.3, both type I and type II non-linear business cycle models will be discussed.

The major difference between the Frischian approach and the deterministic non-linear approach is that, in the former, the fluctuations are driven by exogenous shocks (with or without serial correlation), whereas in the latter they are essentially endogenous, in the sense that the dynamic path is determined by the economic model. In non-linear models, the endogenous fluctuations include the possibility of limit cycles, as well as chaos and the multiperiod cycles, which are discussed further below. Limit cycles may be stable or unstable, but only the former can serve as an equilibrium motion. If a model has a stable limit cycle solution, then the natural, equilibrium, motion of the economy is cyclical. The path that the economy traverses is endogenously determined by the model and is independent of initial conditions. In this case, the role of random shocks is merely to add irregularity to the observed fluctuations; which need not by symmetric in the manner of sine of cosine waves, and which could well have asymmetric expansion and contraction phases. Indeed, the presence of asymmetry is indicative of non-linearity (Blatt, 1980; Brock and Sayers, 1988), since linear models produce symmetric oscillations (see section 3.4 for further discussion). Thus limit or endogenous cycles are an additional possibility, once the linearity assumption is abandoned, and can potentially explain the observed, somewhat irregular, economic fluctuations.

As mentioned in the introduction, one particular type of non-linear process, deterministic chaos, has drawn increasing attention from economists in the 1980s. Chaos theory offers economists the possibility of modelling economic fluctuations without using random shocks, since a chaos process exhibits random-like fluctuations, even though it is totally deterministic. Consider the well known logistic equation:

$$X_{t+1} = aX_t(1 - X_t), \qquad 0 < X_t < 1, \quad 0 < a < 4. \qquad (3.8)$$

This shows that variable X is a function of its previous value and the parameter a, which determines the steepness of the function. For certain values of a ($a \leqslant 3$), the system is stable, but if the value of a increases past 3, the equilibrium point becomes unstable and the time path exhibits a 2-period cycle (i.e. the time path alternates between two values). Further increases in a produce a stable 4-period cycle, then an 8-period cycle and so on, with the periodicity increasing by 2^n ($n = 1, 2, \ldots$). Stable cycles of length 8, 16, 32, \ldots, 2^n, \ldots successively appear and then become unstable, and this all occurs before a limit point of a, which is approximately equal to 3.75. Beyond that point, the time path enters into a region in which the function can exhibit chaos. In the chaotic region, there can be an infinite number of periodic cycles and an infinite number of initial values that produce an aperiodic time path. Baumol and Benhabib (1989) provide a good description of how complex periodicity and chaos arise.

Equation (3.8) can be used to demonstrate the two most important properties of chaos: aperiodicity and sensitivity to initial conditions. First, as shown in Kelsey (1988), when $a = 4$, an analytic solution can be found. Suppose that X_0 is the initial value of X, and is equal $\frac{1}{2}(1 - \cos(u))$, where u is a real number: then $X_t = \frac{1}{2}(1 - \cos(2^t u))$, and it can be seen that the solution is aperiodic if $u/2\pi$ is irrational. That is, starting from the initial value, the

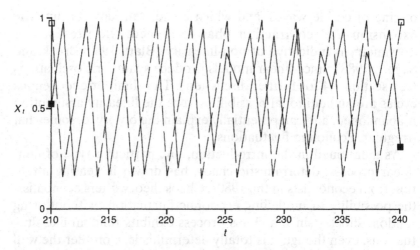

Figure 3.2 Sensitivity to initial conditions.

generated time path will never repeat itself. The second important property, namely that there is a dependence of the time path on initial conditions, is illustrated best in figure 3.2. The motion of equation (3.8) is also sensitive to small changes of the value of parameter *a* (see Butler, 1990). Here the specific equation is $X_{t+1} = 3.8284X_t(1 - X_t)$, with the two initial values (X_0) being 0.101 and 0.100 respectively. The figure demonstrates that a seemingly trivial difference in the initial values can produce a totally different time path after a period of time. Also obvious is that although equation (3.8) is completely deterministic, the behaviour of the system appears to be random.

Clearly, the nature of the fluctuations, particularly the endogeneity or exogeneity of their generations, and their sensitivity to parameter changes and/or to initial conditions or starting values, will have significant implications for the usefulness of the models as forecasting tools, and for the efficacy of macroeconomic stablization policies.

3.3   Non-linear Business Cycle Modelling

To organize the discussion, the non-linear business cycle models developed by traditional Keynesian economists are grouped together, as are the more recent non-linear equilibrium and chaos models. This leaves a miscellany of other non-linear cycle models, which are also discussed in this section.

Non-linear traditional Keynesian models

Hicks (1949), in his discussion of Harrod's (1948) growth theory, observed that the explosive solution to linear deterministic second order difference or differential equations could be employed for cycle analysis. What was required was a ceiling and a floor, in order to constrain the explosiveness. Hicks used the monotonic explosive solution in his multiplier–accelerator model, but it is clear that the cyclically explosive solution or stochastically explosive models would have served equally well. These alternatives would have allowed more variability in the period and amplitude of the resulting cycle.

In Hick's model, which is developed further in Hicks (1950), the ceiling and floor grow at the same (exogenously given) rate as the trend. A positive shock will take that economy away from equilibrium growth via multiplier–accelerator interaction. Once the ceiling is reached, the rate of increase of output slows, and induced investment is reduced to that corresponding to the rate of growth of output along the ceiling. This rate of induced investment is only sufficient to generate a lower level of output, and so output tends to decline; and would continue to fall if the accelerator were to operate in a downward direction. Hicks, however, drops the accelerator (i.e. sets induced investment equal to zero) for the downward path, so that only the multiplier operates. Once the negative multiplier dies not, and is offset by autonomous investment, the accelerator comes back into action, leading to positive induced investment. Expansion takes the economy back to the ceiling, and the cycle is complete and self-perpetuating.

Thus Hicks was able to generate a cycle from the monotonically explosive solution to the multiplier–accelerator model by imposing, in the form of a ceiling and a floor to the economy and an irreversible accelerator, type I non-linearities. Smithies (1957) also develops a multiplier–accelerator model with a type I (discontinuous) non-linearity, which is used to explain both growth and the cycle. A Duesenberry (1949) type ratchet effect on consumption expenditure is used to introduce the type I non-linearity (see also Minsky, 1959).

An alternative approach to non-linear business cycle modelling is to introduce continuous, or type II, non-linearities. One of
the most influential early examples of this approach is Goodwin's
(1951) analysis of the multiplier–accelerator model. The non-
linearity introduced was in the induced investment function, as in
fact had been the case in Hicks (1950). Ichimura (1954), in a
detailed survey of the Keynesian non-linear trade cycle models,
which also develops a synthetic model, compares the induced
investment functions in Hicks (1950) and Goodwin (1951, 1955).

Goodwin discusses a number of models, based on alternative
non-linear investment functions, and demonstrates their potential
to generate limit cycles with expansions contractions of different
length. He also considers the effects on these cycles of introducing
technical progress. The model augmented by technical progress
produces a growth cycle, i.e. a cycle around a growth trend.

Apart from the Hicks and the Goodwin non-linear multiplier–
accelerator models, perhaps the most influential Keynesian non-
linear cycle model is that of Kaldor (1940). Kaldor observed that
the intersection of the savings and investment functions may yield
either stable or unstable equilibria, depending on the relative
slopes of the savings and investment functions. Kaldor postulated
that the savings and investment functions have sigmoid and in-
verse sigmoid shapes, respectively. The intersection of Kaldor's
savings and the investment functions yields three equilibria, two
stable and one unstable. All that is required, in fact, is that one
of the curves be non-linear in the described manner, since the
other could be linear and the three equilibria produced by the
intersection of the linear and non-linear curves would be qualitatively similar.

The cycle resulting from Kaldor's model may be described as
follows. Kaldor argues that the equilibria A and B (figure 3.3,
stage I) are stable only in the short run because, as activity continues at either of these points, forces gradually accumulate which
render them unstable. This is because $I(x)$ and $S(x)$ both assume
constant capital stock, and hence real income, at any particular x,
where x is the level of economic activity. However, these factors
change over time, and $I(x)$ and $S(x)$ will shift accordingly. At high
x (point B, figure 3.3, stage I), the level of investment is high so
that the capital stock (k) is increasing, and so is the output of
consumer goods. The $S(x)$ curve will, therefore, shift upwards,

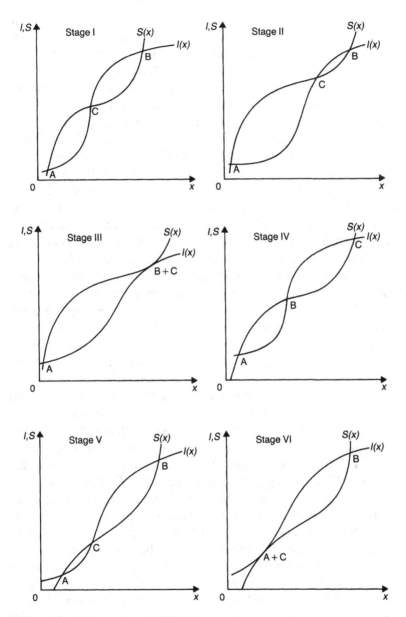

Figure 3.3 The stages of Kaldor's cycle.

for there is both more saving and consumption for any given x. Also, $I(x)$ will gradually shift downwards, since the accumulation of k, by reducing the range of available investment opportunities, will tend to make investment fall. He notes that new innovations will tend to make investment rise, but assumes that the investment-depressing factors dominate. It should be noted that a secondary multiplier effect might offset this tendency. Consequently, point B is gradually shifted leftward, and C rightward, thus reducing the level of x and bringing B and C closer to one another (see figure 3.3, stage II). The critical point is reached when the $I(x)$ and $S(x)$ curves are tangential (stage III). The equilibrium point B + C is now unstable in the downward direction and stable in the upward direction. After a shock, the level of x will fall rapidly, on account of the excess of *ex ante* saving over investment, until a new stable equilibrium, A, is reached.

If we start at the low activity equilibrium (A), forces will again accumulate to shift the curves but, this time, in the opposite direction. If, at A, investment is insufficient to cover replacement, yielding negative net induced investment, then investment opportunities accumulate and the $I(x)$ curve will shift upward. Kaldor notes that this tendency is likely to be reinforced by new inventions. Furthermore, the gradual decumulation of capital, in so far as it reduces income per unit of activity, will cause $S(x)$ to shift downwards over time. Kaldor notes that, even with negative investment, real output could rise due to the introduction of more 'capitalistic' processes of production during the depression, causing a rise faster than $S(x)$. These movements cause A to shift rightwards and C leftwards until a tangency A + C is reached. This new equilibrium is stable in a downward direction, and is unstable in an upward direction. Thus, following a shock, an accumulation will result, coming to rest at B. Thereafter the curves return to the position of stage I, and the cycle is then repeated.

The route followed from B + C to A. or A + C to B, Kaldor claims, might be either along $I(x)$, or along $S(x)$, according to whether *ex post I* is adjusted to *ex post x*, or vice versa. He also suggests that the fall from B + C to A need not be very rapid, because entrepreneurs and consumers take some time to adjust their scale of purchases to their changed rate of earnings. If the process is prolonged, the curve will have shifted back to stage IV by the time A is reached.

Kaldor's non-linear cycle theory had attracted a great deal of interest. It is discussed and compared with the Hicks (1950) and Goodwin (1951) models in Ichimura (1954). The conditions under which it yields a unique limit cycle are discussed by Chang and Smyth (1970) and Lorenz (1989). Klein and Preston (1969) and Kosobud and O'Neill (1972) discuss the stability of the resulting limit cycle in a stochastic context. Varian (1979) applies catastrophe theory to the model in order to prove the existence of a limit cycle, and considers the model as a basis for both a theory of recessions and a theory of depressions. Finally, Schinasi (1981, 1982) considers the model's investment function within an IS–LM framework. All of these contributions utilize the model to explain national income or output, rather than Kaldor's x; which is the level of economic activity measured in term of employment.

Rose (1967) develops a model with a non-linear Phillips curve (as is depicted in figure 3.4), and demonstrates that it has a limit cycle solution. The story of the cycle runs as follows. At the minimum level of E, expected demand prices are rising faster (or falling more slowly) than wages and consequently expected profits induce investment and increase employment. The economy moves up the F–F curve (figure 3.4) towards the flatter region x–x, and once this region is reached there two alternatives: (i) if expected demand price increases still exceed wage inflation, than investment proceeds, employment continues to rise, and the economy moves up the Phillips curve until wage inflation overtakes the expected demand price increases, causing a reversal and a movement back to the flat region x–x; (ii) if, in the region x–x, wage inflation overtakes expected demand price increases, then the economy moves back down the Phillips curve as investment and employment fall. The economy tracks down the curve until wages have fallen sufficiently, relative to expected demand prices, to re-stimulate investment.

We can note that, because the economy can go in either direction, once it reaches the region x–x there is potential in the model for explaining cycles of varying amplitude and period. The variation in this model could be due to variation in the rates of change of expectations, and the analysis would be further complicated by the introduction of price expectations into the Phillips curve. It is clear that the cycle in employment depends critically on the shape of the non-linear Phillips curve being such that it is

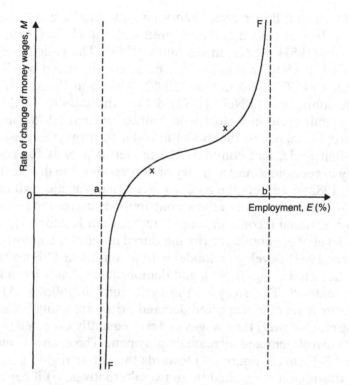

Figure 3.4 Rose's non-linear Phillips curve.

not possible to approximate it linearly or log-linearly, i.e. it must
have a point of inflexion, as was the case for the continuous non-
linear investment function of Goodwin's (1951) model and the
savings and investment functions in the Kaldor (1940) model.
Rose (1969) introduced a money market into his earlier model
and considers the relative roles of real and monetary factors in
determining the cycle. In his alternative analysis of the Phillips
curve, Desai (1973) finds some evidence, in the period 1941–47,
for the shape postulated by Rose. However, its shape was different in the previous and subsequent periods analysed.

  Day and Shafer (1985, 1987) and Day and Lin (1992) develop
non-linear deterministic models derived from the 'standard'
Keynesian model, with 'Robertsonian lags' developed by Mezler
(1941), Modigliani (1944) and Samuelson (1947). These models

are capable of producing multiperiod cycles and 'chaos' solutions, and will be discussed further below.

Miscellaneous non-linear business cycle models

Goodwin's (1967) paper was another highly influential contribution to the non-linear business cycle literature and stimulated numerous extensions, keeping interest in non-linear cycle modelling alive in the 1970s. His model employed a pair of non-linear equations, namely the Volterra–Lotka equations, which were developed to analyse the symbiosis of predator and prey populations. Goodwin, however, used them to analyse the conflict between labour and capital. The mathematics of the Volterra–Lotka equations and the conditions under which they yield conservative oscillations and can be amended to give stable limit cycle solutions are examined by Samuelson (1967, 1971) and Lorenz (1989). The key variables in Goodwin's model are the share of wages in national income (and therefore the distribution of income between workers and capitalists) and the level of employment (unemployment). All profits are invested, so a low share of wages leads to high profit, investment and growth and falling unemployment. The share of wages rises with employment, and investment and growth will eventually decline, and so on. The result is a cycle around a growth trend; hence Goodwin calls it a growth cycle. As such, it is related to the theories of dynamic economic development, but the growth in Goodwin's model is generated by exogenously determined steady (disembodied) technical progress and a steady growth of the labour force. Therefore, growth and the business cycle are not integrated to form a single dynamic process in the manner envisaged by Marx (1867), Schumpeter (1934, 1935, 1939) and Shackle (1968).

Desai (1973) extended the Goodwin class-conflict model by introducing wage–price adjustment, cyclical variation in the capital output ratio, and an (adaptive) expectations augmented Phillips curve. The effect of introducing inflation is to complicate the wage bargaining process, and it has a stabilizing influence unless workers are able to incorporate actual wage inflation into their wage demands. Desai and Shah (1981) reconsider the model under a reformulated technical change relationship which incorporates the Kennedy–Weizaker technical change frontier (Samuelson, 1965).

In Goodwin's model, each side in the class struggle has only one weapon. Workers can bargain on the strength of employment levels, while capitalists can determine growth of employment by their investment decisions. In the Desai and Shah model, capitalists are given an additional weapon; the choice of the induced rate of technical change. This leads to a stable solution, rather than a perpetual cycle as in Goodwin's original model.

Papers presented at an international symposium (held at Siena, Italy in March 1983) were published in Goodwin et al. (1984) and included a number of further extensions of the Goodwin growth cycle model (see also Akerlof and Stiglitz, 1969; Pohjolu, 1979; Velupillai, 1979) as well as other contributions to the theory of fluctuating growth. The symposium rejected, as analytically unsatisfactory, the simple superposition of fluctuations on growth trends because, it was argued, fluctuations and growth interact in a crucial way. Instead, it advocated that a general theory of fluctuating growth be pursued. A central view of the symposium was that economic fluctuations are a natural, endogenously determined, consequence of the internal dynamic structures and conflicts inherent in capitalist economies, and that advanced capitalist economies undergo fluctuations whether or not there is state intervention. Linear models were rejected as inadequate and judged incapable of representing the complex relationships inherent in capitalist economies. The symposium judged the two keystones to an understanding of why capitalist economies evolve cyclically as having been provided by Marx, who stressed class conflict, and Schumpeter, who emphasized the role of technical progress. Goodwin's (1967) growth cycle model had brought these two elements together and spawned a series of studies on Marx/ Goodwin cycles. These are listed in Goodwin et al. (1984).

Van der Ploeg's (1984) contribution to the symposium was to consider the effect of introducing endogenous technical progress, based on Kaldor's (1957) technical progress function, and allowing workers to save and to receive dividends from share ownership. Goodwin (1967) had assumed that workers consumed all their income. The implication of the analysis is that the class conflict, and with it the cycle, is likely to die away as workers obtain an interest in capitalism.

Di Matteo (1984) considers the implications of introducing money into the Goodwin model, and this enables him to examine the interplay between real and monetary factors. Two cases are examined. In the first, the money supply is assumed to be exogenously determined, and it is found that the share of profits is inversely related to the rate of growth of the money supply. If it can control the money supply, the central bank can have a profound effect on the cycle and can, in fact, adopt a rule to eliminate it if certain initial conditions are satisfied. In the second case, it is assumed that the central bank sets the interest rate rather than the money supply and, again, if certain initial conditions are satisfied, the central bank can adopt a rule to eliminate the cycle. Di Matteo stresses, however, that the analysis is highly abstract since it incorporates no theory of the behaviour of the banking sector. Such a theory is necessary to faciliate an analysis of the interplay between financial and industral capitalists in the Schumpeterian tradition (see Mullineux and Peng (1993) for further discussion).

The symposium includes other interesting extentions of Goodwin's model. Glombowski and Kruger (1984) examine the effects of introducing unemployment benefits, while Balducci et al. (1984) use the theory of non-co-operative differential games to explain the effects of introducing the rational expectations hypothesis (REH) into the model. Balducci et al. find that the cycle remains under the REH. This indicates that the cycle is due not to myopia but to the fundamental conflicts inherent in economic development under capitalism, which the model tries to capture. In an attempt to move away from the high level of aggregation, which he finds unsatisfactory, Goodwin's contribution was to analyse economic interactions within the framework of multisectoral models. The multisectoral approach has subsequently been developed by Goodwin, and is discussed further in Mullineux and Peng (1992).

Chiarella (1986) analyses a model (which is closely related to that of George and Oxley, 1985) with a non-linear demand for money function which is dependent on the expected rate of inflation. Initially, the money market is allowed to adjust sluggishly, with inflation expectations being formed adaptively. Chiarella shows that the model has a stable limit cycle if the expectations time lag is sufficiently small. By allowing the time lag to go to zero, perfect foresight is considered as a limiting case. It is found that the stable limit cycle persists. Apart from providing an additional demonstration that plausible non-linear functions can result in a stable limit cycle, Chiarella is able to cast light on the dynamic instability problem that arises because perfect foresight, in the sense that rate of change variables such as inflation can be correctly perceived, leads to saddle point instability. The introduction of a non-linearity removes the instability commonly associated with linear perfect foresight models by replacing the unstable local saddle point equilibrium with a global stable limit cycle equilibrium.

To conclude this subsection, Varian's (1979) contribution is considered. Varian employs catastrophe theory to examine a variant of Kaldor's (1940) non-linear model (discussed in the previous subsection). Catastrophe theory was developed by Thom (1975) (see also Zeeman, 1977) to describe biological processes and has since been widely applied (see George (1981) for another application in economics). Catastrophe-theoretic models consist of a system of differential equations in which the parameters are not constant but change at a much slower rate than the state variables. There are, therefore, essentially two sets of variables. The 'fast' (or state) variables can be regarded as adjusting towards a short-run equilibrium and the 'slow' variables (or parameters) as adjusting in accordance with some long-term process. Catastrophe theory, therefore, studies the movement of short-term equilibria as long-run variables evolve, and would appear to be a particularly useful tool for business cycle analysis and the study of dynamic economic development. When a short-run equilibrium jumps from one region of the state space to another, a catastrophe is said to occur. Catastrophes have been classified into a small number of qualitative types, the simplest of which is the 'fold catastrophe'. This occurs when the system contains one 'slow' variable and one 'fast' variable. For a given value of the slow variable, the fast variable adjusts to a stable equilibrium. If the state space contains 'bifurcation points', at which there are abrupt changes in stability characteristics (as in the Kaldor model), then adjustment to a locally stable equilibrium can involve jumps or catastrophes. Things naturally become more complicated as more fast and slow variables are added. With one fast variable and two slow variables, for example, 'cusp catastrophes', which allow jumps and then either fast or slow returns to short-term equilibria, can occur.

Using a cusp catastrophe, Varian shows that if there is a small shock to one of the stock variables in the Kaldor model, a story emerges that is similar to that analysed using the simpler fold catastrophe, and an inventory recession of minor magnitude results. If the shock is relatively large, however, wealth may decline sufficiently to affect the propensity to save, and a depression can result because the recovery can take a long time. This is related to the idea, discussed in Leijonhufvud (1973), that economies operate as if there is a 'corridor of stability', within which small shocks are damped out but large shocks are amplified. Large deflationary shocks may, for example, produce financial crises and waves of bankruptcies which throw a normally stable system into a deep depression.

Varian suggests that catastrophe theory might usefully form the basis for some further business cycle research. Goodwin (1987) has employed catastrophe theory, and related ideas drawn from bifurcation theory, for analysing dynamic economic development and his work is discussed further in Mullineux and Peng (1993).

Non-linear equilibrium models displaying endogenous fluctuations and chaos

The rapidly growing literature in this area has recently been surveyed by Scheinkman (1990) and Boldrin and Woodford (1990). Introductions to the mathematics of chaos, in (approximately) ascending levels of complexity and detail, are given by Butler (1990), Baumol and Benhabib (1989), Kelsey (1988) and Frank and Stengos (1988a). Some of these references also give partial reviews of the literature on non-linear equilibrium models and the empirical evidence relating to chaos and non-linearity, reviewed in section 3.4.

Boldrin and Woodford's (1990) survey of equilibrium models displaying endogenous fluctuations and chaos is perhaps the most thorough and focused. They concentrate on literature that shows that endogenous fluctuations (whether periodic or chaotic) can persist in deterministic equilibrium models underpinned by microeconomic foundations, in which agents optimize with perfect foresight. They divide the literature into two classes: models with a unique perfect foresight equilibrium, which have perpetual fluctuations for most initial conditions, and in which it is clear that the forces that bring about a competitive equilibrium also require the economy to exhibit endogenous fluctuations; and models in which the perfect foresight equilibrium is indeterminate and which include, among the large set of possible equilibria, ones in which the state of the economy oscillates forever. In the latter class, the forces that generate a competitive equilibrium do not require perpetual fluctuations to occur. The first class consists largely of non-linear growth models (NGMs) and the second class consists largely of overlapping-generations models (OGMs). Given the thoroughness of their survey and parts of aforementioned surveys (Kelsey (1988), for example, also devotes a section to OGMs, while Scheinkman (1990) concentrates more on NGMs), we shall confine our discussion to a few representative examples. Before we proceed, however, we should mention that economic fluctuations can also be modelled as 'sunspot' equilibria. Kelsey (1988) observes that this approach is related to non-linear dynamics because the existence of a 2-period cycle implies the existence of a genuinely stochastic (sunspot) equilibrium (discussed further below).

An early contribution to the NGMs class of models was that of Day (1982), who applies the mathematical theory of chaos to show that, in the presence of non-linearities and a production lag, the interaction of the propensity to save and the productivity of capital can generate growth cycles that exhibit a wandering, saw-toothed, pattern, not unlike observed aggregate economic time series. These 'chaotic' fluctuations need not converge to a cycle of regular periodicity and are not driven by random shocks. Periods of erratic cycling can be interspersed with periods of more or less stable growth. Under such circumstances, the future of the model solution cannot be anticipated from past realizations. A deterministic single equation model is found to be consistent with structural change and unpredictability. Day's work indicates that even if there is substance to the ('Monte Carlo') hypothesis that there are no regular business cycles (Fisher, 1925), economic fluctuations may still be present, and random shocks may not be as important for driving cycles as the Frischian approach implies. (See Mullineux (1990, section 1.2) for a review of evidence pertaining to the 'Monte Carlo' hypothesis.)

Day's results were derived using a modified discrete time version of the Solow (1956) neoclassical growth model. Boldrin and Woodford (1990) review subsequent work using more general optimal growth models. Benhabib and Nishimura (1985), for example, consider a two-sector growth model, in which an optimal cycle of period 2 exists, and Boldrin (1986) goes on to show that cycles of every period, as well as chaos, may arise in the same class of two-sector models. Cycles can also occur in continuous time versions of optimal growth models. Magill (1979) developed a model with damped cycles, and Benhabib and Nishmura (1979) introduced discounting, which added to the persistence of the oscillatory motion, and were able to prove the existence of limit cycles using bifurcation theory.

These non-linear growth models, therefore, produce complex fluctuations which are endogenous equilibrium phenomena, and are market driven. The introduction of market imperfections makes the conditions under which endogenous fluctuations can occur less stringent. Bewley (1986) shows that borrowing constraints can make endogenous cycles possible in a growth model and Woodford (1988a) develops this approach.

The second class of models identified by Boldrin and Woodford (1990) are OGMs with finite-lived consumers. In these models, endogenous cycles and chaos again occur as equilibrium phenomena in the presence of complete and perfectly competitive intertemporal markets. However, in this case the equilibria involving perpetual deterministic fluctuations are a subset of a large set of rational expectation equilibria, which also includes convergence to a steady state. The importance of the OGM class is that, in the 1980s, it stimulated the renewed interest in the endogenous cycle hypothesis by providing the first general equilibrium examples of the chaotic economic dynamics. The papers that have had the most impact are those of Benhabib and Day (1982) and Grandmont (1985).

Of the two, the Grandmont (1985) paper made perhaps the greatest impression: it not only produced complex dynamics from a deterministic equilibrium model, but it also showed that changes in the money supply were non-neutral under rational expectations (perfect foresight), in contrast to the results derived by the New Classical School using (log-)linear models (e.g. Sargent and Wallace, 1975, 1976). This highlighted a point made earlier (Persson, 1979; Dickinson et al., 1982) that the ineffectiveness of monetary policy under rational expectations relies very heavily on the assumptions that the economy can be modelled (log-)linearly and with an additive error term. In Grandmont's model, the equilibrium output depends negatively on the equilibrium level of the real rate of interest, and the nominal rate of interest is shown to be an extremely effective instrument of monetary policy. It is shown that a simple deterministic countercyclical policy can enable the monetary authorities to stabilize business cycles and force the economy back to a unique stationary state (see also Grandmont, 1986).

The source of Grandmont's endogenous deterministic cycles is the potential conflict between the effects of wealth and intertemporal substitution, which are associated with real interest rate movements. Business cycles emerge when the degree of concavity of the traders' utility function is sufficiently greater for older than younger agents. This follows from the assumption that older agents have a higher marginal propensity to consume leisure within the simple structure of an OGM. Grandmont's analysis implies that cycles of different periods will typically coexist. He feels that his results suggest that economic theorists should look more closely at the sort of mechanisms that might be responsible for significant non-linearities in the economic system, if they wish to have a proper foundation on which to build a sound business cycle theory. He postulates that relaxation of the *ad hoc* Walrasian continuous market clearing assumption and the introduction of imperfect competition may lead to the sort of non-linearities that give rise to endogenous economic fluctuations. It would also reduce reliance on variations in real interest rates through variations in relative prices by allowing quantity adjustment, and thus mechanisms akin to multiplier–accelerator effects, to play a role. A sound Keynesian, or non-Walrasian, business cycle theory could than be developed. This, he argues, might form the basis of the 'New Keynesian' business cycle research programme, although most contributions have so far tended to conform to the linear Frischian approach (see Greenwald and Stiglitz, 1987). Grandmont also discusses conditions under which his model could generate a chaotic output.

Versions of the OGM with price uncertainty have genuinely stochastic ('sunspot') equilibrium (Shell, 1977; Azariadis, 1981; Azariadis and Guesnerie, 1986). Azariadis and Guesnerei investigate the relationship between the conditions under which sunspot equilibrium and cycles of order 2 exist in OGM models.

They note that the meaning of sunspot equilibria remains open to interpretation. Their existence demonstrates that competitive markets can be subject to purely speculative fluctuations, driven solely by expectations or psychological factors (e.g. Keynes's (1936) 'animal spirits', or manias and financial panics (Kindleberger, 1978)) that are unrelated to 'economic fundamentals' and yet influence the forecasts and actions of economic agents.

Azariadis (1981), for example, considers the possibility that, under uncertainty, business cycles are set in motion by factors, however subjective, that agents happen to believe to be relevant to economic activity. Such factors could include Keynes's 'animal spirits', consumer sentiment, pronouncements of Wall Street gurus, the growth of certain monetary aggregates, or even sunspots – if a sufficient number of people naively believe they influence economic activity, as Jevons (1884, ch. 7) asserted they did. 'Sunspot theories' demonstrate that extraneous or extrinsic uncertainty is consistent and commonly associated with rational expectations equilibria in an aggregate OGM with no price rigidities and continuous market clearing. Azariadis finds that even well behaved economies typically allow rational expectations equilibria in which expectations themselves spark cyclical fluctuations. This is because, if individuals naively believe in indicators of future prices, such as sunspots or perhaps certain monetary aggregates, they take actions that tend to confirm their beliefs. These self-fulfilling prophecies are a source of indeterminacy which augment the multiplicity of equilibria that typically emerge in generalized monetary models with perfect foresight. A significant proportion of the equilibria may result from self-fulfilling prophecies and resemble perpetual cycles. It is also possible that equilibria resembling permanent 'recessions' or permanent 'booms' will result. Azariadis shows that such 'perpetual' and 'permanent' states may unravel if the uncertainty is reduced by introducing contracts, or as a result of the development of financial markets for claims contingent on predictions, which permit hedging. Woodford (1990) examines the effects of introducing a plausible adaptive learning rule, by which agents might seek to learn whether the sunspot variable is useful for forecasting variables of interest to them, to the Azariadis (1981) model.

In the Benhabib and Day (1982) version of the OGM model, the existence of chaotic perfect-foresight equilibria is emphasized.

Rather than assuming the existence of a fixed supply of fiat money, as in Grandmont (1985), they assume that the government lends to finite-lived private consumers, but it turns out that their results on the conditions under which endogenous cycles and chaos are possible are parallel to those of Grandmont (Boldrin and Woodford, 1990).

The Benhabib and Day and Grandmont models have been criticized (Sims, 1986) because they imply that cycles must have periods of 2 or more; which in this context implies that they should last two generations, or approximately 50 years. They would therefore be classified as Kondratief waves (Solomou, 1987) rather than business cycles (see Boldrin and Woodford, 1990, for further discussion). Grandmont (1986) derives conditions under which monetary and fiscal policy can attenuate the cycle in his model. As Kelsey (1988) observes, the countercyclical policy under consideration is, however, somewhat different from what is usually meant by stabilization policy, given that it is 50-year cycles that are being smoothed.

Kelsey (1988) and Boldrin and Woodford (1990) also point out that the perfect-foresight equilibrium is a relevant concept only when regarded as the limit of a disequilibrium 'learning' process. Kelsey (1988) argues that the learning process will influence behaviour of economic variables and that this will feed back on the learning process itself. Feedback loops of this kind are a common feature of the chaotic system, he observes, so that a learning process could cause chaos in otherwise non-chaotic models. Indeed, the learning process is commonly modelled using an ogive-shaped non-linear curve and, to the extent that this is a reasonable representation (Metcalfe, 1984), explicit introduction of learning entails the introduction of non-linearity to a model that might otherwise be (log-)linear. Grandmont (1985) shows that the non-uniqueness and the instability of steady state and cyclical solutions under perfect foresight are replaced by convergence to an equilibrium and cycle stability once a learning pro-cess is introduced, and Grandmont and Laroque (1986) generalize this result.

OGMs with financial constraints introduced have also been investigated (Bewley, 1986; Sargent, 1987, ch. 6). Bewley (1986) shows that endogenous cycles are possible in such models. Woodford (1988a) introduces a cash-in-advance constraint (Lucas and Stokey, 1983) to a model with infinite-lived workers and entrepreneurs, and derives equilibrium dynamics similar to those in OGMs with financial constraints and which can generate endogenous cycles under circumstances that are similar to those considered by Reichlin (1986). Given that models with infinite-lived consumers can produce dynamic outputs similar to those of OGM-based models, and that the period of fluctuation in them bears no relation to human biology, the Sims (1986) critique of the OGMs does not imply that non-linear endogenous cycle models are inherently unrealistic as a class. Furthermore, as Boldrin and Woodford (1990) point out, the 'periods' in models with financial constraints can be reasonably interpreted as fairly short; indeed, too short to correspond to actual business cycles. They conclude that: 'the construction of examples that allow endogenous cycles at "business cycle" frequencies in the case of empirically realistic parameter specifications remains an important challenge for this line of research'; i.e. that of attempting to explain the business cycle as an endogenous equilibrium phenomenon using non-linear deterministic models.

Not all non-linear equilibrium cycle and chaos models fall neatly into the two classes identified by Boldrin and Woodford (1990). Examples include the following. Van der Ploeg (1986) shows that Begg's (1984) non-linear rational expectations model of equilibrium bond pricing can display financial chaos when risk aversion is of the appropriate degree. Pohjolu (1981) shows that a modified version of the Goodwin (1967) growth cycle model displays complex dynamics and chaos. Lorenz (1987) develops a multisector Kaldor-type cycle model with investment demand interdependencies and shows that chaotic trajectories can result. Puu (1986) extends the multiplier–accelerator model to allow for interregional trade and ceilings and floors, imposed via a non-linear investment function, and shows that a limit cycle solution is possible. Finally, Nusse and Hommes (1990) show how chaos can arise in an modified Samuelson (1939) multiplier–accelerator model, due to Gabisch (1984, 1987), and in a modified cobweb cycle model, due to Cugno and Montrucchio (1984). Other discrete non-linear models include that of Stutzer (1980) and those models developed in Gabisch and Lorenz (1987).

As noted above, Day and Shafer (1985, 1987) and Day and Lin

(1992) have developed 'Keynesian' fixed price macromodels with Robertsonian lags (which emphasize the dependence of demand on past income) that can generate multiperiod cycles and chaotic motion under certain parameter values. Day and Shafer (1985) experiment with a couple of specific non-linear investment functions, including a 'Kaldorian' one, to illustrate their general results. Day and Shafer (1987) derive conditions under which the general model in the 1985 paper generates 'chaos', and use a piecewise linear aggregate demand function and a piecewise non-linear model to illustrate.

Day and Lin (1992) provide a more detailed discussion of the economics underlying their Keynesian cycle, in which the expansion is eventually brought to an end by rising interest rates (due to 'tight' money) which discourage further investment. Falling investment leads to a recession and, as a result of a fall in the transactions demand for money, interest rates also fall. This leads eventually to a re-stimulation of induced investment, and so on. A dynamic non-linear deterministic IS–LM model is used to illustrate such Keynesian-type cycles, and its properties are examined under plausible parameter values derived from data from the 1930s, the 1960s and 1970s. The nature of the fluctuation is found to differ in each period. Two-period cycles are found in the first; 2-period cycles with random amplitude are evident in the second; and, in the final period, both erratic periodicity and random amplitude are indicated. The non-linearity is in the investment function, but it is not of the 'Kaldorian' type. Instead, a shift parameter, reflecting the intensity of endogenous (induced) investment demand, is added to the aggregate demand function. The resulting non-linear investment and aggregate demand functions are thus more 'Hicksian' than 'Kaldorian'. Hicksian ceilings and floors are, however, not required because the economy is constrained by the assumption that the money supply is bounded, and this is reflected in a conventional upward-sloping LM curve.

In this section the discussion has largely concentrated on non-linear deterministic business cycle modelling, although it was noted above that Klein and Preston (1969) and Kosobud and O'Neill (1972) have examined the stability of the limit cycle solution to Kaldor's model in a stochastic context. Kosobud and O'Neill's analysis was analytical, while Klein and Preston undertook a numerical investigation using a piecewise linear approximation to the model and 'empirically reasonable' parameter values. More recently, Benhabib and Nishimura (1989) consider an abstract non-linear stochastic equilibrium model with an infinite-lived representative agent and a neoclassical two-sector economy. Unlike Kydland and Prescott (1982) and Long and Plosser (1983), who used simulation methods to investigate the properties of their stochastic equilibrium models, Benhabib and Nishimura examine the properties of their two-sector model analytically. To do so they introduce the concept of cyclic sets and show that, if a deterministic model has stable period-2 cycles, introducing a small stochastic shock will generate cyclic sets. They conclude that their results are only suggestive, but demonstrate that non-linear two-sector models, although clearly a gross oversimplification, are much richer in dynamic possibilities than are one-sector models. They are, for example, able to account for the asymmetries in business cycles which, as Blatt (1980) and Neftci (1984) have observed, can only be generated using non-linear models (see section 3.4 below). Benhabib and Nishimura make a final observation that further research is needed to identify the particular forms of the non-linearities in preferences and technology that can generate the observed asymmetries within the equilibrium business cycle framework.

3.4 Empirical Evidence of Chaos and Non-linearity

The development and application of chaos theory has not only shed new light on non-linear dynamic modelling but also raised a crucial issue. Can these chaotic or non-linear business models be subject to empirical testing? Unfortunately, the available statistical and econometric techniques are not yet sufficently well developed to allow these models to be tested directly. In the meantime, economists have tried to test whether evidence can be found for the presence of chaos and non-linearity in macro-economic time series. This is important, because only if such evidence is found can non-linear business cycle generating models be taken seriously. In this section, we review the empirical evidence of chaos and non-linearity in macroeconomic data.

Empirical evidence of the presence of chaos

It is known that observed time series generated by chaotic processes appear to be random when investigated using conventional time series methods, such as time series plots, autocorrelation functions, and spectral analysis (Brock, 1986; Ramsey et al., 1990). The current methods of testing for chaos are taken directly from the natural sciences. Since this is not a survey of technicalities (for a survey of non-linear time series models in economics, see Mills, 1991a), in what follows, the basic ideas underlying the two most widely used methods (estimation of correlation dimension and the largest Lyapunov exponent) are discussed. Other methods include the computation of Kolmogorov entropy and some preliminary analysis methods, such as phase space portraits and long-term autocorrelation function plots (see Barnett and Chen, 1986; Frank and Stengos, 1988a).

Before proceeding, it is helpful to introduce the embedding theorem of Takens (1983). Suppose that a time series of real numbers $a_{t_{t-1}}^{\infty}$ which has a *smoothly* (i.e. at least C^2) *deterministic* explanation, i.e. there exists a system (h, F, x_0) such that $h : R^n \rightarrow R, F : R^n \rightarrow R^n$ are smooth and

$$a_t = h(x_t), \quad x_t = F(x_{t-1}), \quad t = 1, 2, \ldots, \quad x_0 \text{ given.} \quad (3.9)$$

(A map or function is of order C^2 if its second partial derivatives exist and are continuous, and is of order C^∞ if all its partial derivatives exist and are continuous.) The equation $x_t = F(x_{t-1})$ can be thought of as an unknown law of motion of an unknown state variable. Nature knows F, but the observer does not. However, measurements $(a_t = h(x_t)$, where h is a measuring apparatus) can be observed. Takens (1983) shows that if one considers *m-histories*

$$a_t^m \equiv (a_t, \ldots, a_{t+m-1}) = (h(x_t), \ldots, h(F^{m-1}(x_t) \equiv J_m(x_t))) \quad (3.10)$$

with a large enough m, the behaviour of the sequence x_t can typically be mimicked by that of the m-histories. Consequently, the empirical test can be simplified dramatically by testing whether evidence of deterministic chaos can be found for the observed m-histories.

As illustrated in figure 3.2, an important property of chaotic motion is its sensitivity to initial conditions. To measure this property, Lyapunov exponents, which characterize the nature of the wandering behaviour of chaotic orbits, are used. Consider an infinitesimal n-sphere with a radius $p(0)$ at time $t = 0$. The sphere will become an ellipsoid as the dynamic system evolves. The ith one-dimensional Lyapunov exponent (λ_i) can be defined in terms of the length of the ellipsoidal principal axis $p_i(t)$, i.e.:

$$\lambda_i = \lim_{t \to \infty} \frac{1}{t} \log_2 \frac{p_i(t)}{p_i(0)}, \tag{3.11}$$

where the λ_i are ordered from the largest to the smallest. It is clear that the Lyapunov exponents are related to the expanding or contracting nature of different directions in phase space. The negative Lyapunov exponents contract the system, while the positive ones stretch the system. If the system's dynamics are chaotic, there will be at least one positive Lyapunov exponent, which characterizes the exponential divergence of orbits from nearby initial conditions. Of particular interest is the sign of the largest Lyapunov exponent. In practice, economists have used an adaption of the Wold et al. (1985) algorithm and the algorithm due to Kurths and Herzel (1987) to estimate the largest Lyapunov exponent.

Another important property of chaotic processes is that they have finite and fractal dimensions, but random variables have infinite dimensions (Brock, 1986; Barnett and Chen, 1988). The definition of dimension is such that a point has zero dimension, a line has one dimension, a plane has two dimensions, and a cube has three dimensions. Consider an infinite sequence, $\{x_t\}$, $t = 1, \ldots,$ ∞, of uniform random numbers on the $[0, 1]$ interval. In line with the above, if $\{x_t, x_{t+1}\}$ is plotted in a two-dimensional space, it will fill the space and if $\{x_t, x_{t+1}, x_{t+2}\}$ is plotted in a three-dimensional space, it will fill the cube. It can therefore be seen that random numbers have infinite dimension in the limit. A major difference between a chaotic process and a truly random process is, therefore, that the former has low dimension while the latter has high dimension. Thus the computation of dimension for a time series is intuitively a method of testing for the presence of chaos. The most suitable measure of dimension for economic application is the correlation dimension (Grassberger and Procaccia, 1983a,b). To define the Grassberger and Procaccia correlation dimension, we first define the correlation integral $C_m(e)$ as:

$$C_m(e) = \#\{(i,j) : \|a(m)_i - a(m)_j\| < e, \quad 1 \leqslant i,j \leqslant N_m,$$
$$i \neq j\}/(N_m^2 - N_m), \tag{3.12}$$

where $N_m = N - (m - 1)\tau$ is the number of m-histories that can be produced from a sample of size N with time lag τ, and $\#A$ denotes the number of distinct points in (cardinality of) the set A. The correlation integral is also called the correlation function, since it measures the correlation of points along an orbit. Changing e changes the number of neighbouring points that are included in the correlation integral, $C_m(e)$. For a completely random series, it is expected that new neighbours are included from each of the m degrees of freedom. If for a time series proportionately fewer new neighbours are included when e is increased, then the time series has a dimension which is less than m. Grassberger and Procaccia (1983a) show that $C_m(e) \sim e^D$, so that D becomes the notion of dimension. Formally, the Grassberger and Procaccia correlation dimension of the m-histories is defined as

$$D_m = \lim_{e \to 0} \lim_{N \to \infty} (\log_2 C_m(e)/\log_2 e). \tag{3.13}$$

Furthermore, at sufficiently small e and large N, it was shown by Grassberger and Procaccia that the correlation integral can be approximated in the form

$$\log_2 C_m(e) = \log_2 k + D_m \log_2 e, \tag{3.14}$$

where k is a constant. Therefore, D_m can be defined alternatively as

$$D_m = \lim_{e \to 0}(\partial \log_2 C_m(e)/\partial \log_2 e) \tag{3.15}$$

The practical implementation should be as follows. First plot $\log_2 C_m(e)$ as a function of $\log_2 e$ for a series of increasing values of m, and then look for the existence of a linear region at low to intermediate values of $\log_2 e$. If a linear region exists, the value of the slope of that linear segment is used as $D(m)$. Two points should be noted. First, at sufficiently low values of $\log_2 e$, the slope will reach a plateau, but at even lower values of $\log_2 e$, noise will dominate and produce further variation of the slope. Secondly, for a well defined chaotic model, the value of $D(m)$ will attain its limit (saturate) at some finite level of m, called the saturation embedding dimension m_s, and the correlation dimension of the strange attractor then is $D(m_s)$. However, if the data are white noise, saturation is never attained, i.e. $D = \infty$ for white noise.

There are some pitfalls in applying the above-mentioned procedures, taken from natural sciences, directly to economic data. First of all, as Brock (1986) points out, many economic time series are generated by near-unit root processes (Nelson and Plosser, 1982), and near-unit root processes can generate low-dimension estimates (see also Sayers, 1990). To see this, consider an AR(1) near-unit root process $z_{t+1} = bz_t + \varepsilon_{t+1}$, where b is near one, $\{\varepsilon\}$ is independent and identically distributed as $N(0,\delta^2)$, and the standard deviation of the stationary distribution of $\{z\}$ is one. Since $\{\varepsilon\}$ is $N(0,\delta^2)$, $\{z\}$ is distributed as $\{N(0,\delta^2/(1 - b^2)\}$: that is $\{z\}$ has been scaled so that $\delta^2 = 1 - b^2$. Since b is near 1, the variance of the error term is near zero. Hence the data points of $\{z\}$ will lie close to a line and the estimated dimension would tend to be one. This possible unit root trap highlights the importance of the Brock (1986) 'residual test' and the 'shuffle diagnostic' used by Schienkman and LeBaron (1989).

Brock's residual test is based on a striking property of chaotic equations – invariance to linear transformations. If one carries out a linear transformation of chaotic data, then both the original and the transformed data (residuals from the linear regression) should have the same correlation dimension and the same Lyapunov exponents. It follows that, if a low-dimension estimate of the original series is not confirmed by the residual series, the original series may well not be chaotic. The basic idea behind the 'shuffle diagnostic' is that if a series possesses chaotic structure, the shuffling process (by sampling with replacement) will destroy it. In other words, the correlation dimension estimate of the shuffled series would be much higher than the dimension estimate of the original series (see Scheinkman and LeBaron (1989) for further discussion).

Furthermore, to obtain reliable results from applying the above-described procedures, large data sets (possibly numbering in the tens of thousands) are required (Ramsey et al., 1990). In economic applications data sets usually consist of less than 1000 observations (especially for macroeconomic time series). Consequently, statistical procedures designed in the natural sciences may not be appropriate in the economic applications. Indeed, this is the main reason why Ramsey et al. (1990) conclude that, for the time series examined so far, there is virtually no available evidence for (or against) the presence of simple chaotic attractors (we return to this point later).

Despite the above caveats, there have been some attempts to test for the presence of chaos in macroeconomic data. Brock and Sayers (1988) carried out extensive tests of various US macroeconomic time series. Their results from applying the residual test are not supportive of low-order deterministic chaos. Scheinkman and LeBaron (1989) examined data on US stock prices. A dimension of about six was found on a weekly index of stocks, and reshuffling the data raised the dimensionality. Therefore, their results suggested the presence of chaos in the time series. Sayers (1986, 1987) investigated man–days lost due to work stoppages and obtained results which are consistent with low-dimension chaos. Barnett and Chen (1988) examined some US monetary aggregates and found evidence of low correlation dimension (1.3–1.5) in log-linear detrended Divisia monetary aggregate series. They did not, however, conduct the residual test or the shuffle diagnostic to avoid the possible unit root trap. Frank and Stengos (1988b) assessed Canadian macroeconomic time series by estimating the correlation dimension and using the shuffle diagnostic. Their results suggested that low-order deterministic chaos does not provide a satisfactory characterization of the data.

The above results seem to suggest that although mixed evidence has been obtained, there is evidence supportive of the presence of chaos in some macroeconomic time series. However, as Brock and Sayers (1988, p. 77) warn, 'This conclusion is too quick!' In the light of the results of Ramsey and Yuan (1989a,b), Ramsey et al. (1990) re-evaluated the calculation of dimension utilized in Barnett and Chen (1988), Sayers (1986, 1987) and Scheinkman and LeBaron (1989). Their results suggest that there is virtually no evidence for the presence of simple chaotic attractors. Furthermore, they argue that biases are created in the dimension estimation process due largely to small sample size and incorrect assumptions about the distribution of the 'error term'. Therefore, the fact that data sizes are small in economics (compared with that of experimental data) seems to pose a serious problem for economists seeking to obtain reliable results in testing for chaos.

Empirical evidence for non-linearity

Because of the problems encountered when testing directly for chaos, economists are paying increasing attention to testing for non-linearity in empirical data. Non-linearity is a necessary, although not sufficient, condition for chaos, and the presence of non-linearity in macroeconomic data has its own implications for macroeconomic modelling, as explained in earlier sections.

There are several methods for testing for non-linearity in economic data (see Mills, 1991, section 5, for further discussion). A widely used method is the BDS test (Brock et al., 1987). The BDS procedure is based on the correlation dimension and the recently developed U-statistic theory for a weakly dependent process (Sen, 1972; Serfling, 1980). Under the null hypothesis that the true model for data is a linear model with independent and identically distributed (i.i.d.) innovations, the following statistic is considered:

$$W_m(e,T) = \sqrt{T} D_m(e,T)/b_m(e,T), \quad D_m = C_m - [C_1]^m, \quad (3.16)$$

where b_m is an estimate of the standard deviation under the i.i.d. null hypothesis. It can be shown, under the null hypothesis, that $W_m \to N(0,1)$, as $T \to \infty$. The detailed derivation of the statistic and the formula for estimating b_m are given in Brock et al. (1987). Note that the BDS procedure does not provide a direct test for non-linearity, however, since the sampling distribution of the test statistic is not known (either in finite samples or asymptotically) under the null hypothesis of non-linearity. The asymptotic distribution is, however, known under the null of independence. Nevertheless, as Brock et al. (1987) show, their test can, using the residuals of a linear model, detect misspecification caused by a linear model fitted to non-linear data. Therefore, the test procedure is as follows: first fit a best linear model to the detrended data; then use the W statistic to test the null hypothesis that the estimated residuals are asymptotically i.i.d.

It should be emphasized that the BDS test has a higher power than that possessed by the conventional time series analysis methods, such as spectral analysis and autocovariance analysis, which find it difficult to distinguish between signals emitted by chaotic models and white noise models (see Brock and Dechert (1988) for detailed discussion). In this sense, the BDS test is a significant new contribution to the field of statistics.

Another widely used method for testing for non-linearity is the family of bispectrum tests (Subba Rao and Gabr, 1980, 1984; Hinich, 1982; Hinich and Patterson, 1985). These tests go beyond the autocovariance function and traditional spectrum analysis to test for 'whiteness', Gaussianity (normality), independence and non-linearity by using the bispectral skewness function. The bispectrum will, for all frequency pairs, be constant for a linear filter applied to pure white noise which is not necessarily Gaussian (normally distributed), and will be zero for a linear filter applied to Gaussian white noise. The advantage of the bispectrum approach is that it provides a direct test for non-linearity as well as a direct test for Gaussianity. However, for testing for independence, Brock et al. (1987) show that the *W* test appears to be more powerful than that based on the bispectrum.

The empirical evidence concerning the presence of non-linearity in macroeconomic time series obtained using the above two methods, and using other methods (discussed below), has been much less controversial than that for chaos. The evidence obtained so far is generally supportive of the presence of non-linearity in macroeconomic data. Using the BDS test, Brock and Sayers (1986) found some evidence of non-linearity for the US investment and unemployment data, although they failed to find evidence for deterministic chaos. Ramsey et al. (1990) find virtually no evidence for chaos, but they admit that there is evidence, of varying degrees of persuasiveness, of non-linearity in all of the data they examined. Indeed, Scheinkman and LeBaron (1989) find strong evidence against the hypothesis of i.i.d. in aggregate US stock returns. They even find evidence against i.i.d. after taking out unit root and ARCH (Engle, 1982) effects. This suggests that extra structure, which is not captured by ARCH models or stationary linear models, exists in their data set. Scheinkman and LeBaron (1987) also investigated annual real GNP *per capita* for 1870–1986 and monthly postwar industrial production for the US. The BDS test suggests non-linear structure in the industrial production. Using the bispectrum test, Barnett and Hinich (1990) find evidence of strong non-linearity in Divisia monetary aggregates, at least at one level of aggregation. This result is consistent with that obtained by Peng (1991) who, using the BDS test, finds evidence of strong non-linearity in Divisia monetary aggregates for the UK.

There are some other studies which test for non-linearity in macroeconomic data using other methods. Using a non-parametric testing procedure, Neftci (1984), for example, investigates whether business cycles are asymmetric, in the sense that contractions are steeper than expansions, and hence non-linear (Blatt, 1980; Mullineux, 1990, section 1.3). Neftci (1984) finds evidence of this type of asymmetry in postwar quarterly US unemployment variables. This is consistent with the result obtained by Brock and Sayers (1986) for that series. De Long and Summers (1986) find little evidence of asymmetry in US time series, apart from unemployment. They argue that Neftci's statistical procedure is inadequate (see also Sichel, 1989) and that asymmetries, which are generally of little significance, are probably the result of the presence of trend growth in many series. They conclude that if proper account were taken of the trend, little evidence of cyclical asymmetry would remain. This, of course, assumes that the trend (growth) and the cycle are separable phenomena. Additional results on asymmetry are presented in Neftci (1986) and Neftci and McNevin (1986); but see Rotemberg (1986) for comments on Neftci (1986), and Falk (1986), who finds little evidence of asymmetry in a number of US series. Mullineux (1990, section 1.4) reviews some of this literature in more depth.

In summary, although there is much controversy regarding the presence of deterministic chaos in macroeconomic data, the evidence for the presence of non-linearity is much more persuasive. This raises serious doubts about the adequacy of modelling macroeconomic time series using linear or log-linear models, and thus has important implications for business cycle modelling. More specifically, non-linear business cycle models (especially stochastic non-linear, or noisy chaotic, models) should be given more serious consideration. Unfortunately, the currently available testing methods cannot reveal the non-linear structures that appear to be present in the empirical data. At this stage, as Brock and Sayers (1986) note, what can be said is that once evidence of non-linear structure is found it is worth spending resources trying to identify and estimate it. Indeed, this is an important future research agenda for economists. The time has come seriously to question the validity of the Frischian approach to business cycle modelling.

3.5 Summary

This chapter has considered the implications of dropping the linearity assumption commonly adopted in business cycle modelling and evidence for the existence of non-linearity in economic time series. In the light of the analysis the following observations can be made.

- Non-linear economic models display a much wider range of dynamic solutions that the (log-)linear stochastic models that have dominated the postwar business cycle literature. Perhaps most importantly, they raise two additional possibilities: first, that the cycle is endogenously determined and, therefore, the natural equilibrium motion of the economy – rather than a response to repeated shocks which disturb the tendency of the economy to converge on a stable equilibrium growth path; and, secondly, that complex dynamics, including multiperiod cycles and chaos, can be generated. In this case the output of the non-linear deterministic model can be irregular cycles or seemingly random series, not unlike macro- and microeconomic time series. In neither case are shocks to the economy the driving force of the economic fluctuations we call business cycles. Furthermore, the same model can have stable, oscillating and chaotic solution paths, according to the initial conditions and the parameter values. If shocks do impinge upon the model, and particularly if they do so in a multiplicative way, causing changes in parameter values, then they may, however, cause abrupt qualitative changes in dynamic behaviour. The role of shocks is therefore different in non-linear models from that assumed in the linear Frischian approach to business cycle modelling.
- If non-linearity is in fact widespread amongst economic relationships, then the importance of the late-1980s literature on the decomposition of time series (into trend, seasonal and cycle components) and on the identification of the main sources of shocks (e.g. real or monetary) is called into question. This is because the analysis is based on linear econometric techniques, the trend and the cycle(s) may not be separable, and shocks may merely add to inherent irregularity, rather than drive the cycle (see Mullineux, 1990, for further discussion).
- The evidence on the existence of non-linearity is generally supportive, but the shortness of data series makes it virtually impossible to undertake powerful tests for chaos in economics. It should be noted, however, that it is linearity that is unusual

in the natural and biological sciences. However convenient it might be, it would be extremely surprising if all economic relationships were linear, as Zarnowitz (1985), in his wide-ranging survey of the business cycle literature, notes. The onus of proof, therefore, lies with the propounders of the linearity hypothesis. Apart from the analytical and statistical convenience of the linearity approach, mainstream economic theory, particularly many neoclassical results (see Mirowski, 1990) and the New Classical money neutrality results, relies heavily on the linearity assumption for its validity.

In the next chapter the literature on political influences on monetary and fiscal policy-making and the business cycle is reviewed. Once such influences are acknowledged, alternative endogenous, and in some cases equilibrium, explanations of the cycle become available and new sources of non-linearities, such as discontinuous policy changes following elections, are revealed.

4

Political Business Cycles, Reputation and Credibility

4.1 Introduction

The two previous chapters have considered the way in which, first, optimizing behaviour on the part of economic agents and, second, the presence of non-linear aggregate economic relationships, can generate the pattern of macroeconomic time series data which is commonly observed. This chapter analyses the role which a major player in the economy, the government, can play, and how interaction between policy-makers' preferences and actions and the behaviour of individual economic agents can explain cyclical patterns in the aggregate economies of democracies.

It was noted in chapter 2 that Gordon (1986) had dismissed the rational expectation with misperceptions (MBC) approach to business cycle modelling in his introduction to an NBER volume entitled *The American Business Cycle*. The 'political business cycle' (PBC) approach was also implicity declared dead because it was hardly mentioned in the volume. Rumours of the death of the PBC approach have, however, proved to be much exaggerated. In the second half of the 1980s there has been a considerable resurgence of interest in the influence of the polity on the economy. Nordhaus (1989) and Alesina (1988, 1989) provide surveys of this literature.

Nordhaus (1975) was primarily responsible for stimulating a flurry of interest in 'political business cycles' in the late 1970s. Other influential contributions were those of Lindbeck (1976) and MacRae (1977). Nordhaus cited Kalecki (1943) as the antecedent of his theory, although Akerman (1947) seems much more closely related. Akerman analysed relationships between economic and political events, considered the view that economic events affected political events, but concluded that political events caused economic events. He analysed electorally induced economic cycles using data from the UK, the US, Germany and France. Nordhaus's theory also postulates electorally induced economic cycles. In contrast, Kalecki (1947) developed a much more 'political' theory in the sense that the cycle was not conditioned by political institutions, such as the electoral period, but by partisan influences. In Kalecki's theory, which reflects the influences of Marx and Keynes, the state manipulates the economy in the interest of the dominant capitalist class and a cycle in unemployment, not conditioned by the electoral period, results. Feiwel (1974) reviews Kalecki's theory and Mullineux (1984, section 3.3) discusses the related work of Boddy and Crotty (1975).

This chapter considers, in detail, the basic ideas behind the PBC approach. The next section looks at how the concept of rational expectations has affected interpretation of the influence of elections on the economic cycle in the context of the early work on PBC. Essentially, it is necessary to move to an explanation which takes into account the ability of sophisticated voters to interpret what the government's optimum reaction to an impending election is. Reputation and policy credibility are considered in section 4.3. It has been frequently pointed out, and will become clear in this chapter, that the literature on credibility of policy is different from that on the PBC models, and looks at different issues. However, in so far as the government's objective function, and the individual economic agent's (lack of) knowledge of it, plays a major role in generating results from the credibility models, it is important to consider this issue in the context of PBC analysis. In other words, the government needs individuals to believe their policy announcements and to be able to differentiate their policy from that of other competing political parties. Recent developments in PBC models and, in particular, the idea of 'partisanship', are considered in section 4.4. There follows a review of attempts to measure empirically the importance of political factors in influencing the behaviour of the aggregate economy. The final section reviews the theory and empirical evidence with a view to providing a judgement on the state of PBC theory.

4.2   The Electoral Economic Cycle

Mullineux (1984, section 3.3) provides a critical appraisal of the
Nordhaus (1975) and MacRae (1977) models. The key features
of the electoral economic cycle approach are as follows: the government is regarded as a vote share maximizer; vote share depends
on economic performance; the government can manipulate the
economy to improve its vote share; and the median voter theorem (see Tullock, 1976) holds. In the latter connection, a Downsian
(Downs, 1957) view of the policy is taken. Ideological, and
therefore partisan, influence can be ignored since, in the manner
of the Hotelling (1929) analysis of spatial competition under
duopoly, the policies of the two parties (a two-party system is
assumed) will converge (see Mullineux, 1984, section 3.3, and
Peltzeman, 1990, for further discussion).

In Peltzeman's terminology, it is a 'rational ignorance' story.
The 'paradox of not voting', which arises because the rational
agent should perceive that the benefits from voting may be non-
existent or negative, since the influence of a single vote can be
treated as zero and because the costs of becoming fully informed
are not zero, is ignored. Nordhaus captures the 'rational ignorance'
by imposing a decaying memory (amnesia) on the electorate, so
that recent economic events have a stronger influence on voting
behaviour than past events. In addition, he assumes that inflation
expectations are formed adaptively, ensuring that the post-election
inflationary consequences of pre-election booms are not anticipated. Together, the decaying memory and adaptive expectations are implicitly assumed to prevent learning over a series of
elections.

Nordhaus (1989) and Peltzeman (1990) present conflicting views
and empirical evidence concerning the 'rational ignorance' hypothesis underlying the electoral economic cycle models and
survey related empirical work. The other hypotheses underlying
the electoral economic cycle theory are also controversial. The
nature of the government's objective function is discussed further
in section 3.3. The assumption that economic variables influence
votes has been subject to widespread testing, and on balance the
evidence is supportive. Mullineux (1984, section 4.3) briefly reviews
a large body of the evidence, but the literature continues to grow.

The assumption that the government could manipulate the

economy to win elections (along with the 'amnesia' and myopia assumptions implicit in adaptive expectations) flew in the face of the gathering force of the rational expectations revolution. As noted in chapter 2, 1975 also saw the publication of Lucas's equilibrium (monetary) business cycle paper, and in this period the influential Sargent and Wallace (1975, 1976) papers were published. Additionally, in 1977, MacRae demonstrated that if the electorate voted strategically, as an electorate endowed with rational expectations would be expected to do, then the electoral economic cycle of pre-election booms and post-election austerity would disappear, and governments would pursue long-run welfare-maximizing policies, rather than opportunistic ones. The final nail in the coffin was delivered by McCallum (1978), who added electoral dummy variables to an autoregressive equation explaining unemployment, based on the Lucas supply hypothesis (Lucas, 1973), and showed that it did not add to the explanatory power of the equation. This was taken to show that Lucas's equilibrium (monetary) business cycle theory dominated Nordhaus' 'political' theory, and as indirectly supporting the findings of Barro (1977, 1978) in favour of the New Classical hypothesis that only unanticipated changes in the money supply influenced real variables.

By the mid-1980s, however, Gordon (1986) *inter alia* was ready to bury Lucas's MBC, and a resurgence of interest in political influences on macroeconomic policy was under way. Not only did this work introduce rational expectations into political–economic models, but it also built on earlier findings of partisan effects on government behaviour. Using data from a number of countries, Hibbs (1977) demonstrated formally that 'socialist' governments prefer lower unemployment and higher inflation than 'conservative' governments. For the UK, and under rational expectations, Minford and Peel (1982) derived a model and presented evidence showing that Conservative governments have lower inflation targets than Labour ones. More recent evidence on partisan influences on economic behaviour will be reviewed in section 4.5.

4.3 Game Theory, Reputation, Credibility and Optimal Monetary Policy Design

Nordhaus (1975) emphasized the need to take account of the government's objective function when analysing economic policy formulation, while the introduction of rational expectations not only raised serious questions about Nordhaus's electoral economic cycle model but also gave rise to the Lucas (1976) critique. This indicated that policy formulation should be regarded as a game between the government and a rational and responsive electorate. The way forward for the political business cycle approach appeared to be to introduce rational expectations into the model and to develop a game-theoretic analysis. The way forward for the Lucas-type policy game approach seemed to be to drop the assumption that governments aim to maximize a welfare function, and to acknowledge political influences by granting the electorate knowledge of the government's (opportunistic and possibly partisan) objective function.

In this section we outline how game theory has been used to analyse policy decisions modelled as games between government and economic agents. In so doing, we are able to introduce the concepts of policy *credibility* and policy-maker *reputation*. For recent surveys of this literature, see Rogoff (1989), Englander (1991), and Blackburn and Christensen (1989). Neither of these important concepts is directly related to the notion of the PBC, although we will argue that they are linked.

The work on credibility and reputation was a response to the analysis of the time-inconsistency of optimal decisions by Kydland and Prescott (1977). The problem identified by Kydland and Prescott, in the context of policy decisions, is that when economic agents are forecasting the future state of the economy, a key element of that forecast will be the actions of the policy-maker. However, there are many situations in which a policy-maker will find it optimal to deviate from an announced policy once it has been built into agent's expectations. As a result, rational agents will not give any credibility to policy which is time inconsistent, and hence sub-optimal policies are used. The literature in this area has concentrated on monetary policy in the context of a Phillips curve type relationship, where welfare is a function of inflation and output (surprises). We shall use this as an example to illustrate the various strands of the literature.

Consider the case in which the policy has a single-period, objective function

$$V_t = V(\pi_t^{(-)}, Y_t^{(+)}), \tag{4.1}$$

where π_t is the rate of price inflation at time t and Y_t is the level of output at time t. The superscript plus and minus signs on the arguments are those for the partial derivatives. The objective function could represent that of society (higher inflation creates economic inefficiency; in the presence of market distortions greater output is welfare improving); or for an electorally motivated government, where inflation and output are the two factors which determine individuals' voting patterns (a vote function).

The policy-maker can use monetary policy to maximize the objective function, with the expectational Phillips curve providing the constraint. We can write this as

$$Y_t = \bar{y} + \beta \, (\pi_t - \pi_t^e), \qquad (4.2)$$

where $\bar{y}$ is the equilibrium level of output (associated with the natural rate of unemployment), and π_t^e is the expected rate of inflation.

The solution to the game that government plays with economic agents is represented by figure 4.1.

Since rational economic agents know the government's objective function, they know that if $\pi_t^e = 0$ there is an incentive to create unexpected inflation and maximize welfare at point A. Hence they will expect a rate of inflation of π_0 which, given that expectation, is optimal for the policy-maker to set. The time-consistent equilibrium is B. This is welfare-inferior to point C, at which the government sets zero inflation. However, C lacks credibility. If economic agents set $\pi_t^e = 0$, then the policy-maker moves to A.

This example illustrates the Kydland and Prescott time-inconsistency problem. In order to solve it, Barro and Gordon (1983b) used an intertemporal welfare function. Suppose that policy-makers maximize

$$Z_t = \sum_{s=t}^{\infty} V_s (1 + \theta)^{t-s}. \qquad (4.3)$$

Now suppose that economic agents adopt an expectation formation strategy such that:

if $\pi_s = 0$, then $\pi_{s+1}^e = 0$; while if $\pi_s \neq 0$, then $\pi_{s+1}^e = \pi_0$ for all S.

Using the previous example we can calculate Z_t for the two alternative policy options.

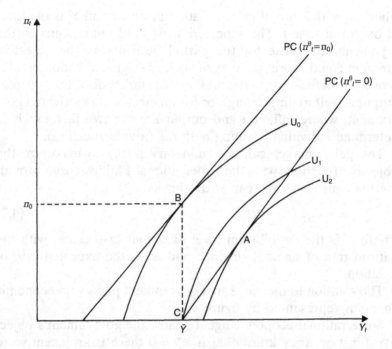

Figure 4.1 The dynamic inconsistency of zero inflation.
U_0, U_1 and U_2 are indifference curves representing the policy-
maker's preferences, with $U_0 < U_1 < U_2$. PC ($\pi_t^\theta = 0$) is the Phillips
curve when expected inflation is zero. PC ($\pi_t^\theta = \pi_0$) is the Phillips
curve when expected inflation is π_0.

For $\pi_s = 0$, the value of Z_s is

$$Z_t^0 = \sum_{s=t}^{\infty} U_1 (1 + \theta)^{t-s}. \tag{4.4}$$

For $\pi_s > 0$, the value of Z_s is

$$Z_t^1 = U_2 + \sum_{s=t+1}^{\infty} U_0 (1 + \theta)^{t-s}. \tag{4.5}$$

Hence we have the solution that π_s will be set equal to zero in all
periods as long as $Z_s^0 > Z_s^1$, and this requires

$$(U_2 - U_1) < (U_1 - U_0)/\theta. \tag{4.6}$$

If this condition holds then a time-consistent zero inflation equilibrium is possible as a result of the reputational equilibrium established.

Barro and Gordon identify two particular problems with this analysis. First, the equilibrium is not unique. Indeed, Barro and Gordon use a slightly different expectations formation mechanism to the one employed here. This point is taken up forcefully by Rogoff (1987). He suggests that the outcome might be different in a repeated game in which agents acted only atomistically but coordinated actions based on government policy announcements. The second problem is that policy-makers are assumed to have an infinite time horizon. This is a requirement, since if they operate on a finite horizon they will always set $\pi_s > 0$ in the last period and, working backwards, the solution therefore collapses. It is difficult to rationalize an infinite horizon when policy-makers are periodically subject to elections.

A method of overcoming this problem is introduced by Backus and Driffill (1985a,b) and Barro (1986). This is to suppose that economic agents are unsure of what the actual objectives of the policy-maker are. Thus, suppose we have two types of policy maker: one (type A) with a welfare function which depends only upon inflation such that they always set $\pi_s = 0$; the other (type B) having the type of objective function used before. In this case, it is straightforward to see that, for the finite time decision period, it is no longer possible to be certain that $\pi_s > 0$ in the last period. Reputation is modelled as the probability of a policy-maker being of type A. As the policy $\pi_s = 0$ is observed by economic agents, they revise upwards the probability of the policy-maker being of type A. As a result expected inflation goes down and the benefits of surprise inflation increase. Hence it may pay a type B policy-maker to play as a type A, in order to build a reputation. This can be represented diagrammatically in figure 4.2.

As the policy-maker plays $\pi_s = 0$, there is a gain in reputation which reduces π_t^e, and the Phillips curve shifts in the direction of the arrows. By consistently playing $\pi_s = 0$, the type B policy-maker achieves welfare levels given by the intersection with the horizontal axis. Hence, once point D is reached, policy-makers of type B are better off than if they had revealed themselves. However, as

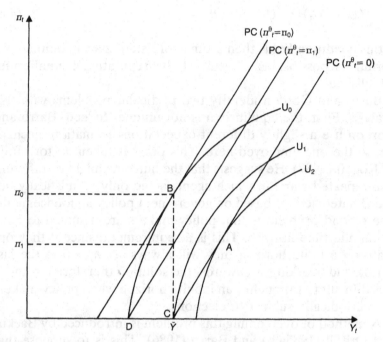

Figure 4.2 Reputation acquisition and policy choice.

the end of the decision period is approached it pays the policy-makers to reveal themselves (i.e. their type), since reputation is unimportant. *When* they reveal themselves depends upon the size of reputation and the temporary gain from losing it, relative to the costs of losing reputation from then on.

The addition of uncertainty about policy-makers' objectives is important both analytically and also in terms of its practical appeal. Clearly, there may be some confusion about what policy-makers are trying to achieve, and hence individuals learn slowly about their intentions. In disinflationary situations this can increase the cost of reducing inflation (e.g., see Anderson, 1989). In circumstances where control over inflation is not exact, there may be an incentive for policy-makers to create further uncertainty so that individuals have less of an opportunity to detect exactly what their motives are (Cuckierman and Meltzer, 1986b). In an alternative view, Canzoneri (1985) considers the case in which the policy-maker has private information which he or she uses benevolently to achieve optimum social welfare. However, economic agents cannot know whether a higher observed inflation rate is due to a poor forecast or deliberate action on the part of the policy-maker. Such an outcome can mean periods during which the low-inflation reputational equilibrium breaks down as a result of a serious mistake by the policy-maker. This is inefficient, and is corrected by making the private information public. These two analyses appear to suggest alternative outcomes, dependent on what the true objectives of the policy-maker are.

The analysis of credibility and reputation does not relate directly to the idea of politically induced policy decisions. However, when the concept of different policy-maker types is introduced, this can be naturally thought of in the context of different political objectives. Similarly, the concept of a termination date for the game is akin to an electoral period, although in the UK, for example, the choice of the election date can become part of the game. There is clear linkage between the two strands of literature.

Some related work on the 'PBC' under rational expectations and asymmetric information is presented by Rogoff (1990) and Rogoff and Sibert (1988). This explores political budget cycles, and is related to Backus and Driffill (1985a,b) in that the government is able to assess its own 'competence' but can only reveal it to the electorate by 'signalling' through the medium of its policy actions. The electorate thereby learns by observing government behaviour. It is not explained how the government can assess its own competence prior to taking office and without itself learning from the public response to its initiatives. The analysis is extended to the case in which the election date is not fixed but can be chosen, as part of the game, by the government within a maximum period (five years in the UK). In this case budget distortions may be less since elections can be called when economic conditions are favourable to the government. Therefore, the government does not always have to engineer such conditions.

While introducing rational expectations and utilizing game theory to analyse monetary, budgetary and fiscal policy formulation, to generate results which – like those of Nordhaus – suggest why governments might be tempted to create pre-election booms, the models discussed in this section studiously ignore partisan influences on policy formulation. The work of Alesina, reviewed in the next section, has no such inhibitions.

4.4 Partisan Cycles

Alesina's (1987) contribution has been highly influential in stimulating widespread recent interest in the 'PBC' and the development of political economic models; an interest that was sustained more by the financial press than economists in the decade or so spanning the above publication and the Nordhaus (1975) publication.

Alesina analyses macropolicy formulation in a two-party system as a repeated game under RE. The model is related to Barro and Gordon (1983) and Kydland and Prescott (1977). Private agents can both vote and set wages in response to government initiatives, and the Lucas supply hypothesis holds. The objective functions of the two parties differ, with one party being more averse to inflation than the other. Variants of the model are analysed elsewhere in Alesina's work. Unless the parties co-operate or reputational forces prevail (in the manner of Barro and Gordon, 1983) the result will be a partial PBC or a 'partisan cycle'. In any event, repeated interaction between the parties (elections) should reduce the significance of the partisan political effects. The 'partisan cycle' involves partisan policies being pursued by the incumbent in the first half of the electoral period and policy convergence in the second half. As Nordhaus (1989) points out, the latter can be interpreted as a switch from ideological to opportunistic (re-election), objections as the election approaches.

Such a switch seems highly likely and could result in a synthesis of the electoral and partisan PBC approaches. Frey (1978) and Frey and Schneider (1978a,b, 1979) recognized a decade or so earlier, however, that a switch need not be automatic. They argued that ideological or partisan policies would be pursued while governments have a safe popularity lead and could be reasonably sure of re-election. Once popularity declines below the safety level (POP*), which was defined to take account of post-election 'honeymoon' periods (and other factors encompassed in the analysis of electoral period popularity cycles), the incumbent party would switch to policies designed to boost popularity and enhance re-election prospects (see Mullineux, 1984, sections 3.3 and 4.3, for further discussion). The switch from partisan to opportunistic policies was not, therefore, automatic but relied on feedback from the electorate about its rating of the government's conduct of policy. A more complex interaction between the economy and the polity was being considered. With the decline of interest in electorally induced economic cycles, interest in the approach pioneered by Frey similarly waned, possibly because Frey also utilized the adaptive expectations-augmented Phillips curve as the basis of his analysis.

Clearly, if partisan cycles are to exist, there must be discernable difference in the policies pursued by incumbent parties of different political persuasion. This underlying hypothesis has previously been tested by Hibbs (1977) *inter alia*, as noted above, and has recently been further scrutinized. This evidence is reviewed in section 4.5, and further evidence is discussed in chapter 5.

Alesina's work has stimulated a significant number of related studies. Alesina's (1987, 1988) model assumes that the electorate knows the objective function of each new government, but that this knowledge is tempered by uncertainty about the electoral outcome, and this introduces political shocks into inflationary expectations. In Backus and Driffill (1985a,b), Cuckierman and Meltzer (1986a,b), Rogoff (1990) and related models, the public has to learn the preferences of the government by observing its policy actions and there is asymmetric information.

Alesina and Cuckierman (1987) make progress towards integrating the two approaches by building a model with 'partisan' parties and imperfectly informed voters. Ellis (1989, 1991) develops an equilibrium partisan model which is driven by political and economic shocks which occur before the election and have asymmetric effects on inflation, unemployment and voting behaviour, depending on which party is incumbent and which variables affect voting. Balke (1991) and Ellis (1991) develop partisan models under the assumption of endogenous voting in the sense that, unlike the Alesina (1987) and related models, the probability of a party winning an election is not independent of its economic policies. In Balke's model, which is related to Alesina (1987), the endogenous election results in the selection of the partisan party best suited to the job in hand. When output is high, the low-inflation party is more likely to win the election, and when output is low, the high-inflation party is more likely to win. The voters' choice of party depends on the state of the economy, and elections function like a state-contingent rule, since voters use their votes to select the party with policies most appropriate to current state of the economy (cycle).

Both Balke and Ellis concentrate on partisanship relating to monetary policy, as did Alesina. Therefore, they implicitly assume government control of monetary policy and a non-independent central bank. In the case of the US, this implies that the nominally independent Federal Reserve Bank responds to the wishes of the Presidential administration. It also suggests that central bank independence might be required to eliminate partisan (and electoral) economic cycles. We shall discuss this issue further in the conclusions to this chapter. As noted above, Rogoff (1990) developed an equilibrium political budget cycle theory devoid of partisan influences. Havrilinsky (1987) attempts to integrate models of fiscal and monetary policy in a partisan model.

Despite the introduction of RE, and the employment of game theory for policy analysis that is consequent upon this as a result of the Lucas critique, one is left feeling that the recent 'partisan cycle' models are not as rich as those developed by Frey (1978) and Frey and Schneider (1978a,b, 1979). As noted above, the latter were flawed in that, like Nordhaus, they assumed an adaptive expectations-augmented Phillips curve, which has subsequently been widely rejected. There have, however, been numerous demonstrations that, under RE, inflation–output and inflation–unemployment trade-offs can exist. There are also numerous other economic policy trade-offs that force decisions upon governments which, in turn, effect the economic well-being of the electorates. What Frey and Schneider were effectively trying to do was to integrate the electoral and partisan approaches, as noted above. The way forward would appear to be to pursue this approach under RE assuming that, in line with Frey and Schneider, the government has a more complex objective function than hitherto assumed in the partisan models. This objective function would combine opportunistic and partisan goals, with switches occurring at critical popularity levels. Incidentally, this would introduce non-linearity (see chapter 3). The government would maximize its objective function subject to both institutional constraints (including the degree of central bank independence recently emphasized by May (1978), who stresses the importance of business interests, and discussed and examined by Frey and Schneider) as well as economic constraints. Not surprisingly, the economics literature has hitherto emphasized the economic constraints. With well defined voter utility functions, popularity (or vote) functions, relating votes cast or voting intentions to economic variables, and policy reaction functions, relating policy instruments to economic outcomes and voting intentions, could be derived and estimated. This would provide for more rigorous testing of the 'PBC' than so far achieved in the papers reviewed in the next section and attempted in chapter 5. However, given differing ideologies and party allegiances, the problem of defining voter utility functions is complex. It is commonly assumed in the partisan literature that high-inflation–low-unemployment policies benefit the 'working classes' and that high-unemployment–low-inflation policies benefit the 'middle classes'. There is some evidence to support this, but it is not that strong and will be discussed further in the next section.

4.5 Empirical Evidence Relating to the 'Political Business Cycle'

Tests of the various theories can proceed by testing the validity of their underlying hypotheses or their predictions. In the former connection, the 'rational ignorance' hypothesis underlying Nordhaus's electoral economic cycle or the absence of 'ultra-rationality' (Nordhaus, 1989) could be tested. Similarly, the behaviour of 'socialist/liberal' and 'conservative' governments could be scrutinized to see if it revealed ideological differences in the manner of Hibbs (1977). All 'PBC' theories, of course, rely on the assumption that economic variables have a decisive influence on voting behaviour and intentions. This literature is not reviewed here, but reviews are provided by Mullineux (1984, section 4.3), Alt and Chrystal (1983) and Hibbs (1987).

Mullineux (1984, section 4.3) reviews evidence on popularity functions, which relate votes cast or popularity ratings to economic variables. It is found that economic variables do significantly affect popularity, at least in some time periods, but there is no general agreement on which variables are the most influential, and there is a strong indication that different economic variables affect popularity to different degrees at different times. In particular, there are switches in the rankings of unemployment and inflation as economic factors causing most concern to the electorate from time to time.

Mullineux (1984, section 4.3) also reviews evidence on policy reaction functions (see also Alt and Chrystal, 1983), which reflect the relationship between government policy instruments and target economic variables. The latter may include economic variables that most influence popularity or which reflect the ideology of the government, such as the distribution of income, or both. Inflation and unemployment have often been chosen because of their influence on popularity, but it should be noted that they also have an impact on the distribution of income. This, in turn, may explain why Labour governments tolerate more inflation and less unemployment than Conservative ones. If both parties have income redistribution objectives, and if unemployment hits Labour voters harder and inflation hits Conservative voters harder, then unemployment and inflation will be key variables. Their influence on popularity may, of course, reflect their influence on the distribution of income.

The key instruments are usually regarded as the money supply or the rate of interest and fiscal variables such as the budget deficit, levels of government expenditure and taxation, and transfer payments. The literature on reaction functions also tests for partisan differences between the major parties (see Hibbs, 1977; Tufte, 1978; Alt, 1979, ch. 7; Minford and Peel, 1982). A major flaw in most of the work is that it does not acknowledge that the reaction functions should be derived from a model in which governments try to maximize their objective functions subject to economic and perhaps other ('institutional') constraints. Those studies that do acknowledge this (Pissarides, 1972; Friedlaender, 1973) use unrealistically simple economic constraints and ignore the implications of the Lucas critique, that a game-theoretic analysis is required if RE is introduced. The general conclusion of Mullineux's review is that there is no general agreement on which instruments and targets are most important, but there is suggestive evidence that policy reactions differ between political parties.

An alternative approach if, as seems to be the case, the underlying hypothesis are not categorically rejected, is to test the prognoses of the rival PBC theories. This has been the dominant preoccupation of the recent empirical literature, and will be reflected in the empirical results that we present in the next chapter. This approach is adopted partly to facilitate a comparison of results for the UK with those of the US, and partly to be consistent with our general time series oriented empirical approach; which aims not to undertake a detailed testing of theories but, rather, to sort out basic issues such as the validity of the linearity assumption and the existence of an influence of the polity on business cycles.

The prognoses can be tested by investigating time series on policy objectives (such as inflation, growth or unemployment) or on policy instruments (such as the money supply, interest rates, transfer payments, tax levels, government expenditure and the budget deficit). This is because the PBC approach hypothesizes that instruments are manipulated to achieve the economic outcomes desired by the incumbent party.

The electoral economic cycle approach has the clearest prediction, and was tested and rejected by McCallum (1978), who added electoral dummies to a New Classical unemployment equation and found that they added no explanatory power. Alt and Chrystal (1983, p. 242) review this and other studies and are struck by the lack of supporting evidence. Hibbs (1987, p. 262) also concludes that evidence to support the hypothesis that US Presidential election years are marked by unusual monetary and fiscal expansions or by short-run surges in output, real income, and employment is not persuasive.

The 'partisan cycle' approach has less well defined testable propositions. Alesina's (1987) formulation does not suggest pre-election booms followed by post-election slumps, giving rise to saw-toothed inflation and unemployment series, as predicted by Nordhaus's electoral cycle. Instead, partisan behaviour can be expected in the first half of the post-election period, followed by consensus policy in the last two years (in the US) prior to an election. This, in turn, contrasts with the Hibbs (1977) type partisan model which predicts that the differences in policy should persist throughout the electoral period. However, it is relatively easy to test for partisan influences using dummies to reflect the years in which each party was incumbent and, indeed, to test for the separate effects of the electoral period and partisan politics using dummies to reflect each influence. This latter approach will be adopted in the next chapter and is also reflected in most of the recent empirical studies reviewed below.

Before this evidence is reviewed, the competing claims of the electoral economic and partisan cycle theories (associated with Nordhaus and Alesina respectively) to represent *the* theory of the PBC has lead to testing of the 'ultra-rationality' hypothesis mentioned above. Nordhaus (1989) presents evidence in support of the hypothesis but, in his comments on the paper, Alesina presents conflicting evidence, and the matter remains to be settled, with both protagonists satisfied that they can rest their case.

Nordhaus (1989) also reviews US evidence supporting the view that fiscal and monetary policy instruments are manipulated, and presents some new supportive evidence. For fiscal policy (taxes and transfer payments) the opportunistic dummy is more significant than the ideological dummy, but both variables make only a small contribution to explaining the growth of transfer payments (contrary to Tufte, 1978). However, social security taxes in the 1960s and 1970s also conform closely to the opportunistic pattern. There have been numerous studies of political influences on the normally independent Federal Reserve Bank. Some try to establish the degree to which it conforms to Presidential policy, implicitly testing the partisan hypothesis that all Republican and all Democrat administrations are alike, and some test for electoral period influences. Nordhaus (1989) briefly reviews this literature. The literature on the non-independence of the 'Fed' is substantial, but the degree and nature of the Presidential influence is still in dispute (e.g., see Kettl, 1986). With regard to opportunistic influences on the Fed's operation of monetary policy, the evidence is mixed. Earlier work by Luckett and Potts (1980) found little evidence to support the hypothesis that monetary policy had been used to generate a cycle in disposable income. More recently, Beck (1984) and Chappel and Keech (1988) found little evidence that the Fed helped to re-elect incumbents by creating pre-election booms, but did find substantial evidence of the Fed adopting the economic goals of the incumbent President. In other words, the partisan influences are found to be significant in both studies, echoing the findings of Hibbs (1977). Grier (1987) tested for an electoral cycle in monetary growth, again using dummy variables, and found a significant pattern of deceleration in the year following the election, followed by accelerating growth in the three subsequent years. This pattern is found to hold for sub-intervals representing different political regimes, implying that it is devoid of partisan influences. Nordhaus (1989) examines changes in the discount rate and finds that the hypothesis of incumbent or party bias on the part of the Fed can be rejected.

Nordhaus (1989) also investigates the behaviour of a target variable (unemployment), using a modified McCallum (1978) test. As noted above, McCallum had found that electoral dummies did not help to explain unemployment. Nordhaus includes both electoral (opportunistic) and ideological dummies and finds them to be significant for most of the period, with the electoral dummy being much larger and more significant than the ideological dummy. In his comments on the paper, Alesina also performs a McCallum-type test by including an electoral dummy and partisan dummies, to represent his 'partisan shock' hypothesis that there are temporary partisan effects following elections, in an unemployment equation. In this case, the temporary partisan effect is fairly significant and the opportunistic dummy is insignificant. Alesina then draws attention to Alesina (1989), which presents similar results for other OECD countries (see also Alesina and Roubini, 1990). In the latter connection, it should be recalled that not all countries have fixed electoral periods.

Chappell and Peel (1979) and Lachler (1982) consider the effects on the electoral economic cycle of treating the election date as endogenous within a game-theoretic model (but ignoring partisan influences). Rogoff (1990) examines the implications of endogenous elections for his political budget cycle. He concludes that fiscal distortions are likely to be less severe for variable-term democracies, because the incumbent can call an early election at an opportune time. This observation would carry over for monetary policy. In a learning context, the desire to call an early election, even if the incumbent is confident that the economy can always be manipulated to create favourable pre-election conditions, could be interpreted as a desire to maintain its stock of credibility or reputation. The incumbent might act opportunistically in choosing the election date because, of course, it cannot be that confident.

The effects of the electoral cycle become less clear under a variable election period, and dummy variables which aim to capture electoral period and, Hibbs-type (full period) and Alesina-type (post-election shock) partisan effects become more difficult to design. This should be borne in mind when evidence from the UK and the US is compared in the next chapter. Keil (1988) applies the McCallum-type dummy valuable analysis to UK data over a 1958–79 sample period. He faces the problem of designing dummy variables to represent electoral influences in the UK. He concentrates on electoral effects on policy instruments, arguing that the choice of election dates when economic conditions are favourable will impart a favourable bias to the influence of dummy variables (chosen *ex post*) on unemployment and other target variables. Therefore, he investigates the impact of the dummy variables on policy instruments, namely government expenditure (the growth rate of real government consumption) and the interest rate. He finds that there is a significant decrease in unemployment and an increase in real output growth rates towards election dates, and a coincident increase in government expenditure; and that the government accommodates wage push pressures if the party in power is unpopular.

Further evidence (for the US) concerning Alesina's 'partisan shock cycle' is presented in Alesina and Sachs (1988) and Alesina (1988). In the latter, using unemployment and an output variable as dependent variables, and including electoral period dummies, Hibbs-type partisan and Alesina-type partisan dummies as explanatory variables, he finds that the results discriminate in favour of the Alesina-type theory of the PBC. Alesina (1988) also presents evidence on electoral and partisan influences on monetary policy, concluding that while there appear to be some partisan influences, the existence of an electoral monetary cycle remains an open question. He also concludes that the evidence presented by Tufte (1978) and in his paper is broadly consistent with a 'political budget cycle' in personal transfer payments. He concludes by suggesting a synthesis between Alesina-type 'partisan shock cycle' models and the 'political budget cycle' models, based on introducing asymmetric information into a partisan game-theoretic model of policy formulation under RE.

Finally, Haynes and Stone (1990) present the results of a series of tests (performed on US data) designed to detect electoral period and partisan influences, and also provide a useful review of previous tests. Rather than rely on electoral period dummies, which they argue are distortionary, they use a sine wave to impose smoothing restrictions on the four-year cyclical variation. They introduce partisan dummies and an electoral partisan interaction variable, which is the product of the partisan dummy and the electoral sine wave variable. GNP estimates support only the electoral model when separate partisan and electoral variables are included, but the addition of the interaction variable leads to dramatically different estimates. In the latter case, it is revealed that the electoral cycle is weaker during Democratic administrations than during Republican ones, in which it is significant. Similar results come through for unemployment and inflation, and it is also evident that output (net of trend) is higher and unemployment is lower in Democratic administrations, while inflation is modestly higher. Haynes and Stone conclude that these results are not fully consistent with Hibbs- or Alesina-type partisan models or the electoral–economic cycle. They find them closest to the Frey and Schneider (1978a,b, 1979) model, which suggests that parties follow partisan policies but switch to re-election policies when popularity slumps, as discussed above and echoed in Keil's (1988) results for the UK concerning monetary policy. During most of Haynes and Stones' sample period (1951–86), the Democrats were the majority party, and were therefore freer to pursue partisan policies, while the minority Republican party was more constrained by electoral concerns. This supports the case, argued above, for developing more complex models, along the lines of the Frey and Schneider approach, but introducing RE and using game theory, to allow for the interaction between the government and the electorate. Such models should permit testable popularity and reaction functions to be derived. This is a suggested avenue for future research and is not pursued in the next chapter, in which dummy variable testing for political influences on economic variables is conducted.

4.6 Summary

This chapter has considered issues of political policy-making and their influence on the behaviour of the macroeconomy. There are a number of points which can be made in this respect.

- The analysis assumes that the authorities can use conventional aggregate demand management to manipulate the economy. The concept of an expectation-augmented Phillips curve lies at the heart of much of the analysis.
- Political factors drive the policy-making process and, when allied to economic agents' reactions to policy initiatives, can provide an explanation for endogenous cycles which involve non-linearities of a discontinuous nature (where the discontinuity is the election date).
- The imposition of rational expectations does not destroy the importance of political factors. Recent work on reputational equilibrium demonstrates that economic agents can be fooled, that additional sources of noise can make the learning process slow and that persistence effects can result.
- The empirical evidence (see also sections 5.4 and 6.2) is supportive of the importance of political policy-making in the behaviour of the macroeconomy, and suggests that it is worthy of further investigation.
- Issues of political influence and the costs of building reputation are indicative of the economic costs of democracy, and provide arguments for taking key policy decisions out of the hands of politicians by, for example, creating an independent central bank (see section 6.3 for further discussion).

5

Empirical Evidence Relating to Business Cycles: New UK Results in Context

5.1 Introduction

The previous three chapters have reviewed theory and evidence on three explanations of cyclical behaviour in the economy. The aim of this chapter is to evaluate each of these explanations for the case of the UK economy since the mid-1950s. In so doing, we hope not only to shed light upon the factors that have caused fluctuations in UK economic activity but also to provide some systematic evaluation of the competing theories. However, because our analysis is only partial in nature we do not claim to provide the definitive answer to these two key questions. First we analyse the statistical properties of the time series for a number of key macroeconomic aggregates. Then we examine a vector autoregressive (VAR) model of the UK economy and consider the sources of shocks which have disturbed aggregate output. Next, we evaluate political influences on macroeconomic variables and the political (electoral) business cycle model. We then report the results of tests for non-linearity in macroeconomic series, and finally we summarize and evaluate the results obtained.

5.2 Non-stationarity and Shock Persistence in UK Macroeconomic Variables

The conventional (Frischian) view about fluctuations (around the growth trend) in macroeconomic variables is that they are driven by unanticipated shocks to the economy. The following question then arises: Do the effects of unanticipated shocks fade away after a reasonably long period of time (i.e. are they transitory), as implied by the Frischian approach; or do they persist throughout the future path of the economy (i.e. are they permanent)? This distinction is important for both macroeconomic modelling and policy analysis. It is at the centre of the current debate (stimulated by Nelson and Plosser, 1982) on whether economic variables in general are best represented by stationary processes around a deterministic trend or by stationary processes around a stochastic trend. In the former case, shocks to output, for example, will have only temporary effects, and thus will not change the permanent component (the long-run growth rate) of output. In the latter case, however, since the shocks are permanent, they affect in varying degrees both the permanent and transitory component (short-run cyclical movements) of the relevant variable. A shock to output would therefore have effects on the business cycle and would simultaneously affect the rate of growth of the economy. For reviews on this debate concerning the US case, see Watson (1986), King et al. (1987), Campbell and Mankiw (1987a,b), Cochrane (1988) and Stock and Watson (1988).

There have been significantly fewer studies of UK macro-economic time series, and most of the reported evidence relates to the nature of the UK output path (e.g., see Walton, 1988; Mills and Taylor, 1989; Mills, 1991). The aim of this section is to provide some new results on the UK case by studying whether the various UK macroeconomic variables, such as output, consumption, investment, the price level and the unemployment rate, are best represented by stationary processes around linear deterministic trends or by stationary processes around stochastic trends. In what follows, we first review the theoretical aspects associated with the notion of non-stationarity and shock persistence, and then present the empirical results, including a test for cointegration.

Non-stationarity and shock persistence

Consider a simple autoregressive model of order one (AR(1)),

$$X_t = \alpha X_{t-1} + \varepsilon_t, \tag{5.1}$$

where ε is a zero mean white noise process of variance σ_ε. By back substitution, this expression can be written as an infinitely ordered moving average process:

$$X_t = \sum_{i=0}^{\infty} \alpha^i \varepsilon_{t-i}. \tag{5.2}$$

Note that ε_t is termed the 'innovation' or shock in X_t, since it corresponds to that part of X_t that could not be anticipated on the basis of the univariate information set available at time $t - 1$. A compactly written version of equation (5.2) is:

$$X_t = A(B)\varepsilon_t, \tag{5.3}$$

where $A(B) = \sum_{i=0}^{\infty} \alpha^i B^i$ is a polynomial of infinite order in the backward operator B (i.e. $B^i \varepsilon_t = \varepsilon_{t-i}$). As noted in Harvey (1981) and Granger and Newbold (1986), stationarity implies $\lim_{i \to \infty} \alpha^i = 0$. Therefore, for a stationary process, the effect of shocks fades over time: that is, stationarity implies transitory shocks, or zero persistence. Macroeconomic variables, such as output, consumption and investment, typically exhibit an upward trend. The conventional practice in macroeconomic modelling of GDP, for example, is to decompose it into permanent and transitory components by regressing its logarithm against a linear time trend. The time trend is used to capture the natural rate of growth, while the detrended series is assumed to be stationary and is interpreted as describing the business cycle.

However, following Nelson and Plosser (1982) and many subsequent studies, there has been a substantial amount of criticism of the aforementioned regression against a linear time trend approach, since empirical evidence often reveals that such detrended series are non-stationary. An alternative approach is to assume that the permanent (trend) component is also stochastic. This accords with the class of *integrated* time series, for which stationarity can only be achieved by differencing. A time series is said to be integrated of order d ($I(d)$) if it requires differencing d times to achieve stationarity. As shown in Nelson and Plosser (1982), many US macroeconomic variables are $I(1)$ processes, the first differences of which are stationary. An $I(1)$ process exhibits a set of properties which are completely different from those of a stationary process. In particular, unlike a stationary process, the shocks to an $I(1)$ process persist forever. To see this, consider the following $I(1)$ process:

$$(1 - B)X_t = \mu + A(B)\varepsilon_t. \tag{5.4}$$

For simplicity, it is assumed that X_t is a random walk with drift, i.e. $A(B) = 1$:

$$X_t - X_{t-i} = \mu + \varepsilon_t. \tag{5.5}$$

The following expression is obtained by solving the above difference equation (a zero initial value is assumed):

$$X_t = \mu(t - t_0) + \sum_{i=0}^{t-t_0}\varepsilon_{t-i}. \tag{5.6}$$

It can readily be seen that each shock ε_{t-i} contributes its full value to X_t, rather than its discounted value $\alpha^i\varepsilon_{t-i}$ ($|\alpha^i| < 1$), as in a stationary process. Therefore, shocks to a random walk will persist forever.

Furthermore, as shown in Stock and Watson (1988), the value $A(1) = \Sigma\alpha^i$ in equation (5.4) can be interpreted as a measure of how persistent shocks to X_t are. For example, $A(1) = 0$ for any trend stationary process, whereas $A(1) = 1$ for a random walk, as shown above. Other positive values of $A(1)$ are possible, depending upon the size and signs of the α^i. In order to gauge how persistent shock to macroeconomic variables are, numerous studies have attempted to estimate the value of $A(1)$ for various macroeconomic variables: see, for example, Campbell and Mankiw (1987a), Cochrane (1988) and Stock and Watson (1998) for the US; and Mills (1991) for the UK. Note that since $A(1)$, as in equation (5.4), is an infinite sum, difficulties arise in estimating it. Several methods have been proposed by economists for estimating $A(1)$ (see Stock and Watson (1988) for a review). One method is based on approximating $A(B)$ by a ratio of finite order polynomials (Campbell and Mankiw, 1987a). Specifically, if it is assumed that the first difference of X_t (ΔX_t) is a linear stationary process, then it follows that it has an ARMA(p,q) representation:

$$\phi(B)\Delta X_t = \theta_0 + \theta(B)\varepsilon_t, \tag{5.7}$$

where $\phi(B) = 1 - \phi_1 B - \ldots - \phi_p B^p$ and $\theta(B) = 1 - \theta_1 B \ldots - \theta_p B^q$. Equation (5.7) can be rewritten as:

$$\Delta X_t = \phi(1)^{-1}\theta_0 + \phi(B)^{-1}\theta(B)\varepsilon_t. \tag{5.8}$$

Therefore, $A(B) = \phi(B)^{-1}\theta(B)$, and $A(1)$ can be computed as $A(1) = \theta(1)/\phi(1)$. The above procedure will be used in our estimation of $A(1)$ for various non-stationary macroeconomic variables.

In the next subsection, we first test whether the various UK macroeconomic variables (including both real and nominal GDP, real consumption and investment, the price level and the unemployment rate) are stationary, and hence whether shocks to these variables are persistent. In the case of non-stationarity, we then test whether they are $I(1)$ processes. If so, we then estimate the persistence measure $A(1)$ from a ARMA specification, which is selected on the basis of parsimony (i.e. using as few parameters as appropriate; see Harvey (1990, p. 28)) and test for adequacy using various summary statistics (see below). Finally, we also test whether the real GDP has common stochastic trends with the real consumption, i.e. whether they are cointegrated.

Unit root and cointegration test results

The quarterly series of real and nominal GDP (denoted as RGDP and NGDP, respectively), real consumption (RCON), real fixed capital formation (RFCF), the consumer price index (CPI), the implicit GDP price deflator (GDPP), the change in inventories (STOCK) and the unemployment rate (computed as the ratio of the total unemployment to the workforce) (UNEMR) are investigated. The data source is Data Stream. All series are seasonally adjusted, and the sample period is from 1956.I to 1991.III for all variables except UNEMR, for which the seasonally adjusted data are available only from 1959.I. The logarithms of the series are used in the tests for all variables except UNEMR and STOCK. Note that the data for inventories were available only in changes over time, and hence STOCK can be regarded as the first differences of inventories.

Unit roots tests were performed by computing the Augmented Dickey–Fuller τ_r (for levels) and τ_μ for (first differences) statistics. In all cases two lags of the first differences (for testing whether the levels are stationary) or second differences (for testing whether the first differences are stationary) were included to eliminate serial correlation. The results are presented in table 5.1, which

Table 5.1   Unit roots test results, 1956:I–1991:III

Variables	Levels	First differences
RGDP	−1.84	−7.06
NGDP	−2.01	−13.6
RCON	−2.20	−5.08
RFCF	−1.83	−5.61
CPI	−1.98	−3.39
GDPP	−1.98	−11.96
STOCK	−5.10	—
UNEMR[a]	−3.62	—
Critical values		
1%	−4.025	−3.478
5%	−3.442	−2.882

[a] The sample period was 1959:I–1991:III.

shows that both the unemployment rate and changes in inventories are stationary around a linear time trend. For all the other variables, stationarity can only be achieved by taking the first differences, i.e. these series are $I(1)$ processes. Consequently, shocks to these variables will be persistent. To further gauge how persistent shocks to these $I(1)$ variables are, an $ARMA(p,q)$ model is fitted for the first differences of each variable on the basis of parsimony, and two statistics are used to test for misspecification (see also Mills, 1991a). The persistence measures $(A(1))$ are then computed from the estimated AR and MA co-efficients. The results are reported in table 5.2. Note that the conventional Box–Pierce Q-statistics is based on 12 residual autocorrelations and is distributed as $\chi^2(12 - p - q)$. This statistic is intended to assess the fit of the model to relatively low order autocorrelations. The S-statistic (Gaynon, 1988), which is computed by summing the sample partial autocorrelations from lag $(p + q + 1)$ to lag 24, and is distributed as $N(0,1)$, is designed to test for low-frequency relationships not captured in the models. From table 5.2, several points should be noted. First, both the Q- and S-statistics are insignificant in all the models presented, suggesting that the selected models are reasonably good-fitting

Table 5.2 Estimates of the persistence measure $A(1)$

Variables	(p,q)	$A(1)$	Q	S
RGDP	(0,0)	1.00	14.28	−0.64
NGDP	(4,4)	3.07	6.59	0.08
RCON	(0,4)	0.98	14.84	−0.441
RFCF	(0,0)	1.00	10.93	0.138
CPI	(0,4)	3.34	9.92	0.03
GDPP	(4,2)	3.97	12.58	0.34

specifications. Second, real GDP and real fixed capital formation follow a random walk. This suggests that neither real income nor investment have transitory components. Instead, they consist only of a permanent stochastic component. In other words, all shocks are persistent and there are no business cycles in the two series. This result is consistent with the evidence on the real GDP for the UK reported in Mills (1991a), although he used a data set (1955.I–1986.IV). With regard to the rest of the variables, the persistence measure for real consumption is close to unity; while the estimated $A(1)$ for the nominal GDP, the price index and the implicit GDP price deflator implies that shocks to these nominal variables are highly persistent. Finally, the contrasting results for the real and nominal GDP suggest that the cyclical variation in nominal GDP is the result of cyclical fluctuations in the price level, and the results for RPI and GDPP tend to support this conjecture.

Finally, we use the Engle–Granger methodology to test whether RGDP is cointegrated with RCON, i.e. whether the series have a common stochastic trend so that there exists a long-run stable relationship between the real income and the real consumption. Since real GDP was found to follow a random walk, it coincides with permanent income (Hall, 1978). Therefore testing for cointegration between real GDP and consumption will have implications for the validity of the permanent income hypothesis (Friedman, 1959). Because it is known that the results from the Engle–Granger approach may be sensitive to the choice of the left-hand side variable, we first computed two static regressions with alternative normalized variables:

Table 5.3 Cointegration test results, 1956:I–1991:III

Dependent variable	R^2	D–W	D–F
RGDP	97.3	0.075	−1.46
RCON	95.5	0.076	−1.33

$$RCON_t = c_1 + \beta_1 RGDP_t + \mu_{1t}, \qquad (5.9)$$
$$RGDP_t = c_2 + \beta_2 RCON_t + \mu_{2t}. \qquad (5.10)$$

Using a formal augmented Dickey–Fuller test (as described in Engle and Granger, 1987), the residuals from the above two regressions were then tested for stationarity. The results (presented in table 5.3) suggest that the real income is not cointegrated with the real consumption. This implies that the permanent income hypothesis cannot be accepted.

5.3 A VAR Model of the UK Business Cycle

In this section, we investigate the source of the UK business cycle fluctuations. The model used is essentially an open-economy variant of the models, for the US, of Sims (1980), Blanchard (1986, 1989) and Blanchard and Quah (1989) and, for the UK, of Turner (1991). Specifically, we build a vector autoregressive (VAR) model for the UK economy using a number of major macroeconomic variables. To account for the openness of the UK economy we include, as an extension to Turner (1991), the real exchange rate variable into the model. The variance decompositions and the impulse response functions are then examined, in order to study the effects of different shocks of fluctuations in variables such as real income, unemployment, and price level, and so on. In what follows, we first briefly review the VAR and structural VAR modelling methodology, and discuss the selection of variables in the model as well as other statistical issues such as the importance of stationarity of the variables. The main results on variance decompositions and impulse response functions are then presented.

A VAR model for the UK economy

Vector autoregressions (VARs) were introduced by Sims (1980) as a method of estimating structural macroeconomic models. Consider a structural model of the following form:

$$C_0 X_t = C_1 X_{t-1} + C_2 X_{t-2} + \ldots C_m X_{t-m} + D\varepsilon_t, \qquad (5.11)$$

where X_t is a $p \times 1$ vector of variables, C_i, $i = 0, 1, \ldots, m$, and D are $p \times p$ matrices of coefficients; m is the maximum lag length; and ε_t are the structural innovations, which are assumed to be independently distributed with zero means and diagonal covariance matrix Ω. The reduced form of the system can be obtained by premultiplying both sides of equation (5.11) by the non-singular matrix C_0^{-1}:

$$X_t = \sum_{i=1}^{m} A_i X_{t-i} + e_t, \qquad (5.12)$$

where $A_i = C_0^{-1} C_i$ and $e_t = C_0^{-1} D\varepsilon_t$. Equation (5.12) is the form in which the VAR is estimated, but it is not possible to use the VAR in this form for policy analysis because the innovations to the reduced form depend upon the matrix of contemporaneous relationships among the variables in the system, C_0, and the matrix D. To identify the structural innovations appearing in equation (5.11), so that policy analysis can be conducted, a set of restrictions on the structures of the matrix C_0 and D is needed. Specifically, a set of just-identifying restrictions for equation (5.12) is needed such that we obtain equation (5.11) with ε_t containing a set of orthogonal innovations. Consequently, the impulse shocks to the innovations of an individual equation can be regarded as a shock to a particular structural economic relationship, rather than some combination of relationships, as is the case in equation (5.12). Sims (1980), and other early studies on VAR models, tackled the issue of identification by assuming that the matrix D is diagonal and that the matrix C_0 is lower triangular. The second assumption implies that the system is recursively ordered.

The problem with Sims' approach is that the results can be highly sensitive to the ordering of equations, which tends not to be based upon economic theory. Blanchard (1989) presents a variation of the Sims (1980) model, in which he permits limited simultaneity between the variables (i.e. C_0 is not lower triangular) and some structural disturbances to appear in more than one equation (i.e. D is not diagonal) by imposing additional restrictions on C_0 and D based on economic theory and external information. Turner (1991) presents, for the UK economy, a model which is very similar to that of Blanchard (1989). Neglecting lag terms, Turner's (1991) model can be written as:

$$y = v_d, \qquad u = c_{21}y + v_\pi, \tag{5.13, 5.14}$$

$$p = c_{34}w + c_{31}y + d_{32}v_\pi + v_p, \tag{5.15}$$
$$w = c_{43}p + c_{42}u + d_{42}v_\pi + v_w, \tag{5.16}$$

$$m = c_{51}y + c_{52}u + c_{53}p + c_{54}w + v_m, \tag{5.17}$$

where y, u, p, w and m are output, unemployment, prices, wages and money respectively. The c_{ij} are the ijth elements of the C_0 matrix and the d_{ij} are the ijth elements of the D matrix. Note that wages appear in the price equation, introducing simultaneity between wages and prices. To achieve identification, Turner (1991) borrowed Blanchard's (1989) restriction that $d_{42} = 0.1$. No justification was given for using this information, based on the US economy, for the UK. Smith and Murphy (1991) apply an open-economy variant of the above model to the Australian economy. Specifically, in addition to equations for output, unemployment, real wages and money, they include three equations for world variables, such as world output, terms of trade and world interest rates. Due to difficulties in determining an appropriate ordering of the system, Smith and Murphy (1991) tried different recursive orderings, with the world variable equations always being kept at the top.

We included five variables in our model for the UK economy; the real exchange rate (REX), output (RGDP), the unemployment rate (UNEMR), price level (GDPP) and the money supply (LM4). The real exchange rate for the UK sterling pound against the US dollar was included to account for the 'openness' of the UK economy. The log of money stock (M_4, as defined by the Bank of England) is used as the money variable. All variables are seasonally adjusted, and span the period between 1963.I and 1991.III (because the data for M_4 are available only from the first quarter of 1963), and all but REX and UNEMR are in logarithms. We used the following recursive ordering: RGDP, UNEMR, GDPP, M_4 and REX. Note that our ordering is similar to that used in Turner (1991), except that we add an equation for the real exchange rate. The equation for RGDP represents an aggregate demand curve, with innovations in the equation being interpreted as the aggregate demand shock. The innovations in the unemployment equation represent the labour supply/productivity shocks. The equation for the price level (GDPP) can be regarded as a supply curve, and its error term a cost (supply) shock. Our ordering implies that output, unemployment rate and price variables are present in the money supply equation. The reason for this ordering is that a broad measure of money is used. Its value cannot be perfectly controlled by the central bank and it depends, at least to a certain extent, on surprises in money demand (velocity). Alternatively, one may argue that broad money M_4 includes bank current account deposits which reflect bank credit creation in the form of lending, which in turn is demand led. Finally, we assume that the surprise in the real exchange rate depends on the surprises of all the fundamental variables in the model (e.g., see Dornbusch, 1976; West, 1987), and thus the REX equation is the last one in our model. The residual component of the REX equation may be regarded as reflecting speculative forces of variations in risk premia uncorrelated with the fundamental variables (West, 1991).

Before we report on the formal estimations for the models, note that the assumptions made about the nature of the trend in series are crucial in VAR methodology, since stationarity is required for the results to be valid. To determine whether the levels or first differences of the variables should be used in the estimation, we again (because of different data periods) used the augmented Dickey–Fuller tests to investigate whether the variables have unit roots. The results are presented in table 5.4. The first column in table 5.4 shows that all variables except for UNEMR are non-stationary in their levels. The second column is in line with the results presented in the previous subsection, i.e. stationarity can be achieved for all the non-stationary variables by taking their first differences. On the basis of the above results, we used the first differences for all the variables in the estimation of the VAR models.

Model estimates and simulations

In estimating the reduced form of the VAR, the lag length was set at 5 on the basis of Akaike's Information Criterion for a

Table 5.4 Unit roots test results, 1963:I–1991:III

Variables	Levels	First differences
REX	−2.436	−5.477
M_4	−2.952	−5.114
GDPP	−1.262	−3.450
RGDP	−2.332	−4.942
UNEMR	−3.641	—
Critical values		
1%	−4.042	−4.043
5%	−3.450	−3.450
10%	−3.150	−3.150

multivariate system (see Harvey, 1981, p. 187). The variance decomposition of the model is presented in tables 5.5–9. Throughout the forecast period, the strongest influence on real output is its own structural disturbance, aggregate demand shocks. However, the disturbances in unemployment rate, money, real exchange rate and price equations become more important through time. A notable difference between our results and those of Turner (1991) is that the latter found, in contrast, little impact of productivity shocks coming through the UNEMR equation on real output. For unemployment, the importance of its own disturbances declines quite rapidly, and those of the others, especially demand shocks, increase steadily. For prices, the strongest influence comes from its own (cost) disturbances, and it declines only slowly throughout the forecast period. A notable result is that money supply shock has little impact on prices, while demand shocks and labour supply/productivity shocks play a much more important role. If we look at the variance decomposition of money, we see that, apart from the importance of its own disturbances, the shocks from the price equation play an increasingly important role through the forecast period, while those from the output and unemployment equations have little impact. These results are consistent with our earlier conjecture that (for broad money supply), money velocity shocks such as those from price increases (due to cost shocks), play an important role. In other words, the

Table 5.5 Variance decomposition of RGDP

Period	RGDP	UNEMR	GDPP	M_4	REX
1	100.0	0.00	0.00	0.00	0.00
4	91.18	6.77	0.91	0.53	2.17
8	84.82	9.43	1.55	2.01	2.45
16	83.78	9.75	1.80	2.20	2.47
24	83.60	9.75	1.92	2.23	2.47

Table 5.6 Variance decomposition of UNEMR

Period	RGDP	UNEMR	GDPP	M_4	REX
1	19.09	80.90	0.00	0.00	0.00
4	37.32	55.88	1.72	4.18	0.87
8	39.08	48.77	5.58	4.28	2.27
16	36.46	46.95	8.66	4.05	3.86
24	36.19	46.89	8.93	4.03	3.92

Table 5.7 Variance decomposition of GDPP

Period	RGDP	UNEMR	GDPP	M_4	REX
1	8.52	0.01	91.47	0.00	0.00
4	8.69	3.15	84.02	0.39	2.73
8	7.59	5.17	81.99	1.88	3.34
16	6.99	5.58	80.79	2.81	3.81
24	6.62	4.68	81.48	3.36	3.82

Table 5.8 Variance decomposition of M_4

Period	RGDP	UNEMR	GDPP	M_4	REX
1	0.29	0.83	0.09	98.77	0.00
4	4.94	1.51	0.66	89.36	3.51
8	4.41	2.57	2.97	83.18	6.85
16	4.08	3.11	8.46	75.60	8.73
24	4.07	3.45	11.5	71.98	8.91

Table 5.9 Variance decomposition of REX

Period	RGDP	UNEMR	GDPP	M_4	REX
1	0.28	0.11	0.14	0.02	99.42
4	4.96	1.67	0.46	0.89	92.00
8	7.13	5.59	1.37	1.23	84.65
16	7.26	6.25	2.22	1.48	82.77
24	7.29	6.35	2.40	1.49	82.44

broad money supply cannot be regarded as totally exogenous and under perfect control of the central bank. In the case of the decomposition for the real exchange rate, in addition to its own disturbances, the shocks from aggregate demand and productivity are much more important than those from the nominal factors such as the price level and the money supply.

We now turn to the impulse response functions, which are presented in graphical form in figures 5.1–5. The results are broadly consistent with the predictions of Keynesian macro-economic models. A positive aggregate demand shock of one standard deviation in magnitude lowers the unemployment rate and increases the money demand in the short run. The unemployment rate then increases and the money demand decreases steadily towards equilibrium values. The response of output and unemployment to a monetary shock is consistent with the existence of an upward-sloping short-run aggregate supply curve and a downward-sloping short-run Phillips curve. Here, a positive money supply shock increases output and lowers unemployment in the short run. One puzzling result is that, as in Turner (1991), prices appear to decline during the first year of expansion. Turner's explanation of this is that, assuming that prices are set on an average cost basis, then the initial increase of output due to monetary expansion may induce a price decline, since average costs tend to decrease as fixed costs are spread over a greater volume of output. However, as Turner (1991) admitted, this kind of interpretation can be viewed as an *ad hoc* piece of theory intended to accommodate uncomfortable empirical results. Given

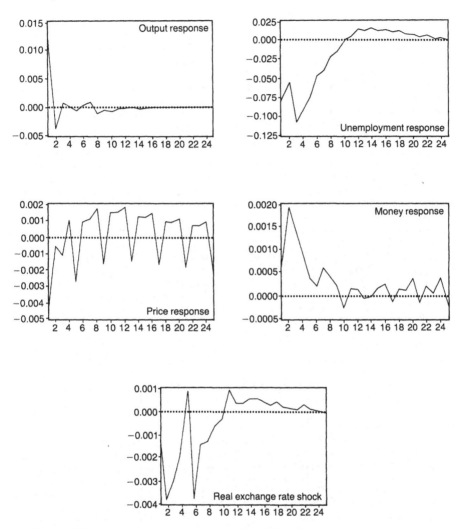

Figure 5.1 Responses to a one standard deviation demand shock.

the openness of the UK economy, it is of interest to look at the effect of real exchange rate shocks to key macroeconomic variables such as output and unemployment rate. In figure 5.5 it is suggested that a real depreciation will increase output and lower unemployment in the short run, with both effects peaking within the first year.

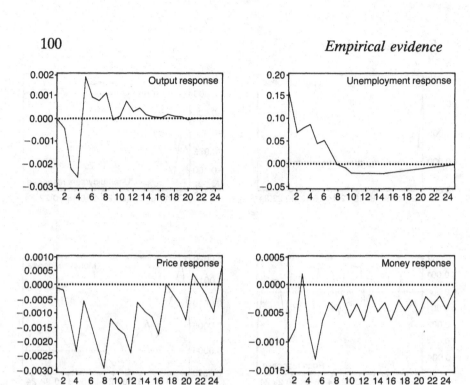

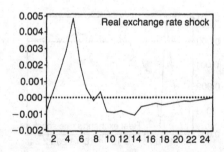

Figure 5.2 Responses to a one standard deviation labour supply or productivity shock.

5.4 Evidence of Political Business Cycles in the UK

In this section, we examine evidence of political manipulation of macroeconomic policy to win elections. As reviewed in chapter 4, the Nordhaus (1975) 'political business cycle' (PBC) model suggested that politicians stimulate aggregate demand before

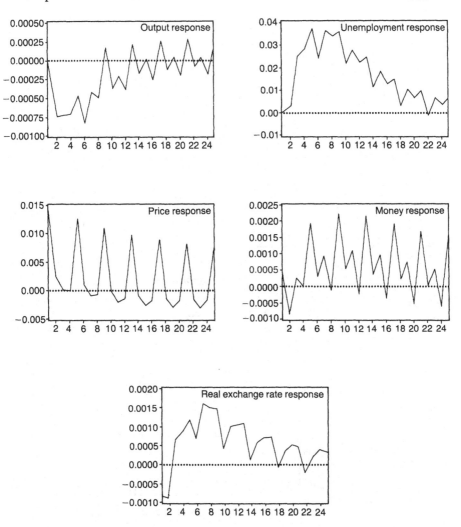

Figure 5.3 Responses to a one standard deviation cost or supply shock.

elections in order to create faster economic growth and reduce unemployment, with a view to maximizing their likelihood of re-election. However, subsequent rational expectation PBC models assert that regular multiyear cycles in GDP or unemployment are very unlikely, but short-run manipulations of policy instruments such as money supply and public debt often occur due to the

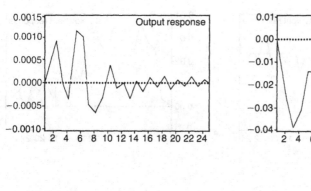

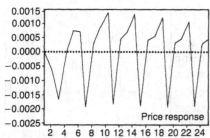

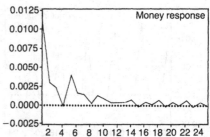

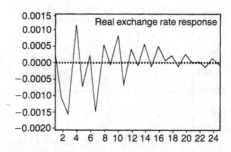

Figure 5.4 Responses to a one standard deviation money shock.

time-inconsistency of optimal plans and exploitation of reputation effects (see chapter 4). We will test for the existence of 'political business cycles' in both economic outcomes and policy instruments for the UK. The data used include quarterly series of real GDP, unemployment, inflation, money supply (M_4) and general government financial deficit (surplus).

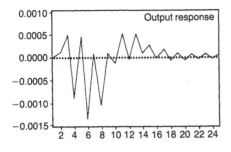
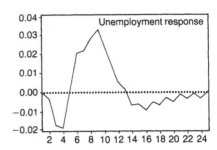

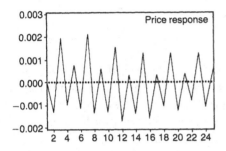
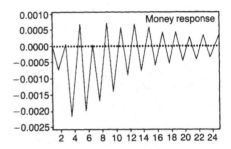

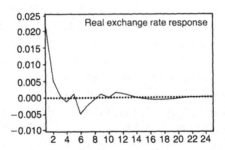

Figure 5.5 Responses to a one standard deviation real exchange rate shock.

Political business cycles in real GDP and unemployment

Following the approach of McCallum (1978), to test for the PBC evidence on the real GDP, we run the following simple but powerful regression:

$$y_t = \alpha_0 + \alpha_1 y_{t-1} + \ldots + \alpha_n y_{t-n} + \beta PBC4_t + \varepsilon_t \qquad (5.18)$$

Table 5.10 Regression on real GDP growth, dependent variable y_t;
1960:I–1991:III

Variables	Coefficient	t-statistics
Constant	0.007	2.33
y_{t-1}	0.698	8.11
y_{t-2}	0.029	0.30
y_{t-3}	0.055	0.57
y_{t-4}	−0.414	−4.25
y_{t-5}	−0.317	3.68
PBC4	0.005	1.22
	$R^2 = 0.52$	

where y_t, the rate of GDP growth, is computed as $(\text{GDP}_t - \text{GDP}_{t-4})/\text{GDP}_{t-4}$, at time t. PBC4_t is a 'dummy' variable which takes a value of unity in the three quarters before an election and in the election quarter, and zero otherwise. The results for the regression on real GDP growth are reported in table 5.10. The autoregressive specification for the dependent variable was chosen on the basis of its autoregressive properties, i.e. sufficient lags were included in the regression so that autocorrelations of the residuals are not statistically significant. Table 5.10 reveals that the political dummy has the sign (positive) which is consistent with the theoretical prediction, but it is insignificantly different from zero.

Results from a similar regression on unemployment rate (U_t) are reported in table 5.11. Based on the unit root test results presented in section 5.2, a time trend variable was included in the regression to tackle the problem of non-stationarity. Again, the political dummy has the correct sign (negative), but is not significantly different from zero. We have also tried slightly different definitions of the dummy variable (assigned the value of unity two and four quarters before the election and in the election quarter, and zero otherwise), and the results (not reported here) were qualitatively similar. Therefore, our results seem to confirm the conclusion reached in other studies for OECD countries (including the UK), such as Alesina (1989) and Alesina and Roubini (1990), which reject the PBC model using GDP and unemployment. Unlike Alesina, however, using dummy variables, we were unable to detect any partisan effects on output, unemployment and inflation, which is considered next.

Table 5.11 Regression on unemployment rate, dependent variable U_t; 1960:I–1991:III

Variables	Coefficient	t-statistics
Constant	−0.016	−0.42
TIME	0.003	3.31
U_{t-1}	1.475	17.24
U_{t-2}	−0.143	−0.89
U_{t-3}	−0.365	−4.09
PBC4	−0.009	−0.21
	$R^2 = 0.98$	

Political business cycle on inflation

As noted in chapter 4, Nordhaus' PBC model suggests that there is a surge of inflation immediately before and/or after the election due to the pre-electoral expansion. The PBC models under rational expectations, such as Rogoff and Sibert's (1988) budget cycle model, also have a similar implication for inflation. The difference is that the latter has no implications for growth and unemployment.

In table 5.12, we display the regression results on the inflation rate. The dummy variable (PBCX) used takes a value of unity in the two quarters preceding and following an election, and in the election, and in the election quarter, and zero otherwise. It is shown is table 5.12 that the dummy PBCX has a coefficient which has the correct sign and is significant at the 10 per cent level. Therefore, our results provide some moderate evidence of electoral cycle in inflation. In summary, our findings in this and the last subsections are not supportive of the Nordhaus model, but are not necessarily inconsistent with models which emphasize cycles on policy instruments. We present the detailed results on the policy instruments in the next two subsections.

Monetary policy and elections

The focus of this subsection is to examine the implications of the opportunistic 'political business cycle' on monetary policy. Partisan dummies again proved insignificant in this case, and also for fiscal policy, considered next.

Table 5.12 Regression on inflation rate, dependent variable π_t; 1960:I–1991:III

Variables	Coefficient	t-statistics
Constant	0.002	0.89
π_{t-1}	1.390	16.07
π_{t-2}	−0.388	−2.63
π_{t-3}	−0.022	−0.15
π_{t-4}	−0.292	−2.02
π_{t-5}	0.278	3.32
PBCX	0.004	1.46
	$R^2 = 0.95$	

First, following Alesina et al. (1992), we computed the following regression:

$$m_t = \beta_0 + \beta_1 m_{t-1} + \ldots + \beta_n m_{t-n} + \gamma \text{PBC4} + \varepsilon_t, \qquad (5.19)$$

where m_t is the annual growth rate of broad monetary aggregate M_4. Note that Alesina et al. (1992) used the narrowly defined monetary aggregate M_1. This became a discredited measure of money supply due to financial liberalization and innovation, because it does not include interest-bearing bank and building society sight deposits. In fact, the Bank of England ceased to publish M_1 series in 1989. PBC4 is the electoral dummy variable used earlier. The PBC theory suggests that the coefficient on PBC4 should be positive and significantly different from zero, implying that money growth is higher immediately before election. The regression results, reported in table 5.13, shows that the coefficient on the dummy variable has the correct sign (positive), but is insignificantly different from zero. One may argue that money supply measured by a broad monetary aggregate depends critically upon other economic variables, such as the growth rate of real income and inflation rate. This is because a large part of M_4 consists of bank deposits which depend upon bank lending. We therefore computed a regression of equation (5.19) including the current and once-lagged annual growth rate of real GDP and the inflation rate. The results, presented in table 5.14, again reveal no

Table 5.13 Regression on money growth, dependent variable M_4; 1963:I–1991:III

Variables	Coefficient	t-statistics
Constant	0.016	2.75
m_{t-1}	1.196	11.99
m_{t-2}	−0.185	−1.21
m_{t-3}	−0.165	−1.08
m_{t-4}	0.035	0.35
PBC4	0.001	0.16
	$R^2 = 0.86$	

Table 5.14 Regression on money growth, dependent variable M_4; 1963:I–1991:III

Variables	Coefficient	t-statistics
Constant	0.010	1.63
m_{t-1}	1.144	11.39
m_{t-2}	−0.138	−0.89
m_{t-3}	−0.137	−1.37
y_t	0.038	0.43
y_{t-1}	0.139	1.46
π_t	−0.119	−1.13
π_{t-1}	0.166	1.55
PBC4	−0.002	−0.50
	$R^2 = 0.87$	

evidence of electoral manipulation of money supply. Our findings are consistent with those reported for the UK in Alesina et al. (1992), but, as noted they used M_1, a narrow measure of the money supply. One possible explanation for the failure of finding evidence of electoral manipulation of money supply is that, as argued above, in a modern monetary economy, money supply is largely endogenous, so that it is difficult or very costly for the government to try to manipulate the growth of money.

Table 5.15 Regression on fiscal surplus/deficits, dependent variable z_t; 1961:I–1991:III

Variables	Coefficient	t-statistics
Constant	−42.608	−0.27
z_{t-1}	0.478	5.09
z_{t-2}	0.301	3.19
u_t	−695.950	−2.36
u_{t-1}	661.618	2.30
y_t	1428.783	0.39
y_{t-1}	1468.369	0.41
PBC4	−194.523	−1.23
	$R^2 = 0.77$	

Fiscal policy and elections

Both traditional and recent 'rational' PBC models suggest that we should observe fiscal expansions before elections. The pre-electoral fiscal expansion can be conducted through either a reduction in taxes or an increase in government spending, or both. An effective approach to examine the election effects on fiscal policy is thus to concentrate on the government fiscal deficits (surplus). Quarterly series of general government financial deficit (surplus) were used. In order to control for the economic determinants of budget deficits, following Roubini and Sachs (1989), we include regression variables derived from the optimizing theories of fiscal deficits (e.g., the 'tax smoothing' model of Barro (1979, 1986) and traditional Keynesian models of fiscal deficits). Both theories suggest that fiscal deficits emerge during periods of recession and growth slowdown, because of, for instance, the automatic stabilizer effect. We therefore include the unemployment rate and the real GDP growth rate in the regression. We tried two dummy variables: one is the PBC4 used earlier, while the other, denoted PBC6, takes a value of unity five quarters before an election and in the election quarter, and zero otherwise. The results are reported in tables 5.15 and 5.16 respectively.

First, note that, since the series of government financial surplus or deficits is used as the dependent variable (z_t), an increase in

Table 5.16 Regression on fiscal surplus/deficits, dependent variable z_i; 1961:I–1991:III

Variables	Coefficient	t-statistics
Constant	−38.129	−0.24
z_{t-1}	0.480	5.14
z_{t-2}	0.0298	3.18
u_t	−685.410	−2.34
u_{t-1}	650.936	2.27
y_t	2337.308	0.64
y_{t-1}	1085.191	0.31
PBC6	−219.987	−1.50
	$R^2 = 0.77$	

government deficits means a decrease in z_t. It can be seen from both tables that the coefficients on unemployment rate and GDP growth rate have the correct signs; that is, a rise in unemployment increases the budget deficit and an acceleration of GDP growth lowers it. The coefficients on both of the dummy variables have the correct signs, one (that on PBC6) being significantly different from zero at 10 per cent significance levels and the other (that on PBC4) on the borderline. Consequently, our results provide some evidence of electoral manipulation of fiscal policy instruments.

The results presented in this section, viewed in the context of the political business cycles literature as reviewed in the last chapter, are broadly consistent with findings in other studies. Specifically, our results do not support the Nordhaus formulation of the PBC, but generally do not reject the 'rational political budget cycles' of Rogoff and Sibert (1988). However, these policy changes do not appear to influence all the variables of interest to the policy-maker, such as output and employment, and we find that partisan dummies are not significant in the UK.

5.5 Chaos, Non-linearity and Macroeconomic Variables

As noted in chapter 3, while business cycles vary in duration and amplitude, one of the common characteristics is that expansions are normally long and slow, and contractions are usually sharp and quick. In other words, the pattern of macroeconomic variables such as GDP, unemployment and investment appears to be asymmetric over time. However, macroeconomic model specifications have, in the main, tended toward log-linear specifications, driven by symmetric, exogenous shocks. In chapter 3, we reviewed efforts to increase our understanding of business cycles by economists who have proposed deterministic chaos models, which are characterized by endogenous instability. This approach has inspired great interest in non-linear macroeconomic modelling, and the detection of empirical evidence of chaos and non-linearity in business cycle data. In this section, we present some empirical evidence of chaos and non-linearity in a group of UK macroeconomic variables. The data used are quarterly series of real gross domestic product (RGDP), real consumption (RCON), real fixed capital formation (RFCF), unemployment rate (UNEMR), consumer price index (CPI) and nominal GDP (NGDP). The sample periods for these series are the same as those in section 5.2. Since the technical details of the test methods can be found in chapter 3, in what follows we concentrate on presenting the results and discussing their implications for macroeconomic modelling.

Detecting chaos in macroeconomic data

As discussed in section 3.4, two major methods have been used by economists in detecting chaos in economic data; computation of the maximum Lyapunov exponent, and correlation dimensions. The Lyapunov exponent algorithms used so far cannot easily differentiate between autoregressive processes (common in economic data) and pseudo-random variables. Both types of stochastic processes can generate spurious positive Lyapunov exponent estimates, and consequently economists have tended towards relying increasingly on estimation of the correlation dimensions (Sayers, 1990). We adopt the same strategy in our investigation. As discussed in section 3.4, near-unit root processes pose a problem in obtaining meaningful estimates of correlation dimensions, and since evidence presented in section 5.2 shows that all series but the unemployment rate are first-difference stationary processes, we will utilize Brock's residual test, described in section 3.4.

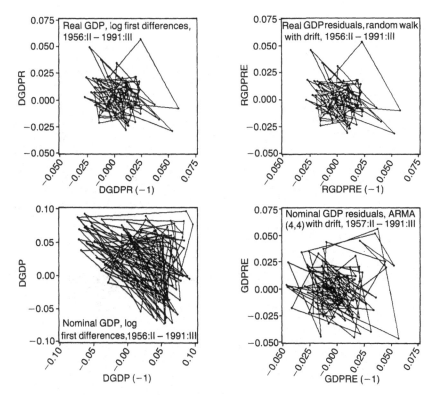

Figure 5.6 Phase portraits I.

On the basis of the results obtained in section 5.2, we rendered our data series time-stationary by taking log first differences, with the exception of the unemployment rate, for which linear time detrending was used. Furthermore, we fitted ARMA(p,q) with drift models (again based on the results in section 5.2) to those log first differences and to the detrended unemployment rate, and obtained residuals of the various regressions. Phase portraits of the log first differences of the various series and detrended UNEMR, and those of ARMA(p,q) with drift model residuals, are given in figures 5.6–8. Note that all figures appear to be quite random, except for the log-linear detrended unemployment rate. However, the phase portrait of the residuals of the ARMA(2,2) with drift model for UNEMR appears to be random. For all other series, the phase portraits of the residuals generally appear to be more random than those of the log first differences. These

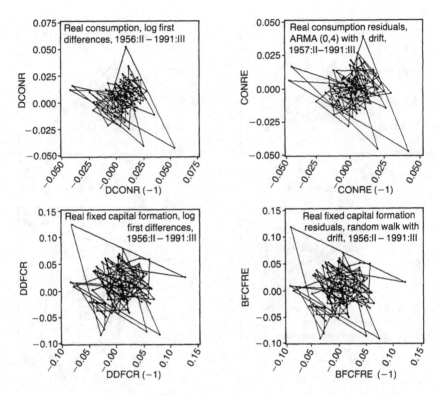

Figure 5.7 Phase portraits II.

graphs suggest that there exist autoregressive and/or moving average structures in the data, and thus it is important to filter obvious linear correlations in the data by fitting ARMA(p,q) models and to scrutinize the obtained residuals in order to test for additional structure.

For the purpose of estimating correlation dimensions, as described in section 3.4, we plot log $C(e)$ versus log e. The GP (Grassberger–Procaccia) plots of the various time stationary series (log first differences, and log-linear detrended UNEMR), and those of the corresponding ARMA(p,q) with drift residuals, are presented in figures 5.9 and 5.10. In order to obtain meaningful estimates of low correlation dimensions, we should observe the following: first, a zone of stability on the plots so that the measurement of the slope within this zone of stability (i.e. the linear region) provides an estimate of the dimension of the data; and,

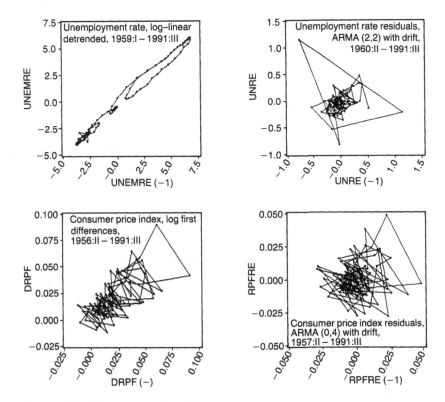

Figure 5.8 Phase portraits III.

second, the dimension estimates for the various embedding dimensions should tend to saturate to a finite level (see section 3.4 for a detailed discussion). Furthermore, for a deterministic chaos process, Brock's residual test should be passed, i.e. the estimates of the correlation dimensions for the residuals should be close to those for the original time-stationary series. It is obvious from the graphs presented that there is insufficient evidence to permit the acceptance of the null hypothesis of determinism.

Detection of non-linear structure in macroeconomic data

Although the hypothesis of deterministic chaos was rejected for macroeconomic data examined in this chapter, the method of estimating correlation dimensions can be turned into useful tests for general non-linear structure in time series data. Specifically,

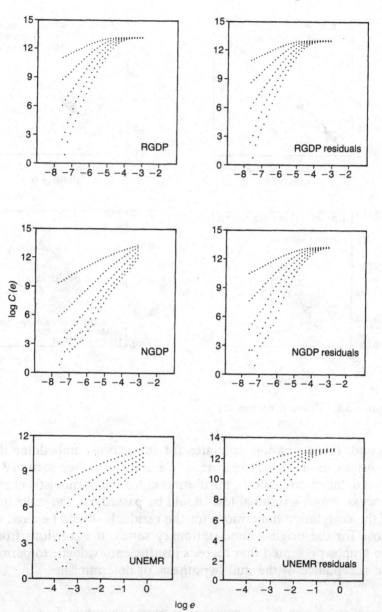

Figure 5.9 GP plots I.

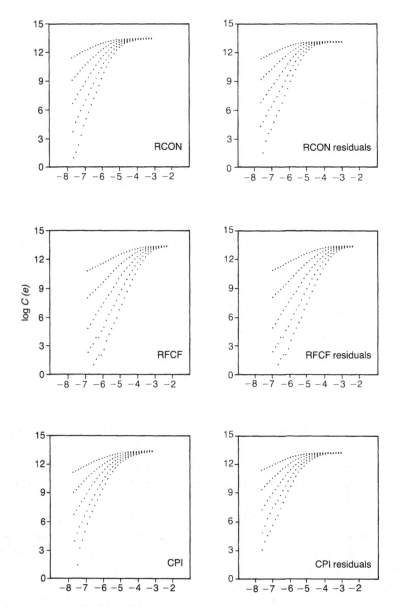

Figure 5.10 GP plots II.

Table 5.17   BDS statistics, real GDP; 1956:I–1991:III

	Log first differences		ARMA (0,0) with drift residuals	
m	C_m	*BDS*	C_m	*BDS*
2	3173	2.13	3174	2.18
3	1814	2.15	1817	2.20
4	1081	2.65	1083	2.69
5	706	3.92	707	3.94

Table 5.18   BDS statistics, nominal GDP; 1956:I–1991:III

	Log first differences		ARMA (4,4) with drift residuals	
m	C_m	*BDS*	C_m	*BDS*
2	2818	2.28	2998	4.33
3	1575	3.63	1802	4.85
4	1039	7.58	1132	5.54
5	891	16.13	740	6.39

the BDS tests the null hypothesis of independent and identically distributed random variables (i.i.d.) against general non-linear structures (see section 3.4). In this subsection, the BDS test is used to detect evidence of any remaining structure in the residuals of time series models.

We calculated BDS statistics for the time-stationary series as well as the residuals of the ARMA(p,q) with drift models. The results are reported in tables 5.17–22. Several observations can be made. First, the BDS statistics for log first differences of fixed capital formation and the residuals of its time series model are all close to zero, suggesting that the series appear to be random, and thus that the null hypothesis of i.i.d. cannot be rejected. The BDS statistics for the log first differences of real consumption are on the borderline, but those for the residuals of its ARMA(4,4) with drift model are close to zero. This implies that the conventional time series model is reasonably good for modelling the real

Table 5.19 BDS statistics, unemployment rate; 1959:I–1991:III

	Time detrended series		ARMA (2,2) with drift residuals	
m	C_m	BDS	C_m	BDS
2	4497	3.79	3592	2.87
3	4302	4.65	2462	2.64
4	4122	5.78	1738	2.84
5	3948	7.45	1231	2.88

Table 5.20 BDS statistics, real consumption; 1956:I–1991:III

	Log first differences		ARMA (4,4) with drift residuals	
m	C_m	BDS	C_m	BDS
2	3463	0.01	3136	0.04
3	2031	0.24	1704	−0.88
4	1222	0.61	958	−0.62
5	721	0.56	554	−0.26

Table 5.21 BDS statistics, real capital formation; 1956:I–1991:III

	Log first differences		ARMA (4,4) with drift residuals	
m	C_m	BDS	C_m	BDS
2	3154	1.21	3154	1.21
3	1751	0.87	1750	0.85
4	919	0.02	917	−0.01
5	500	−0.02	499	−0.03

consumption. Second, the BDS statistics for the other log first difference series and the time detrended unemployment rate are large, leading to rejection of the i.i.d. null hypothesis. This is no surprise, because all of these series contain obvious linear structure. Furthermore, the BDS statistics for the residuals of the time series models for these variables are, in general, smaller than

Table 5.22 BDS statistics, consumer price index; 1956:I–1991:III

	Log first differences		*ARMA (4,4) with drift residuals*	
m	C_m	BDS	C_m	BDS
2	4243	6.29	3431	3.31
3	3023	6.91	2140	3.28
4	2159	6.96	1351	3.25
5	1648	7.96	843	3.03

those for the original time-stationary series, again because the latter contain obvious linear correlation structure. However, the BDS statistics, reveal that the residuals still contain some remaining structure. Finally, it should be noted that the BDS statistics for the log first differences of real GDP are very close to those for the residuals of the time series model. One may argue that this is not surprising because the first differences were regressed only against a constant, based on the random walk hypothesis established in section 5.2. For the purpose of robustness, we also fitted an AR(2) model to the first differences of RGDP, and the BDS statistics for the obtained residuals are 1.32 ($m = 2$), 1.21 ($m = 3$), 1.56 ($m = 4$), and 2.74 ($m = 5$), again indicating some remaining structure in the residuals. In summary, evidence of some degree of non-linearity was found for the real GDP, the nominal GDP, the consumer price index and the unemployment rate.

5.6 Summary

This chapter has presented empirical evidence on the characteristics of business cycles in the UK, using a variety of techniques. The key findings are listed below.

- All variables examined, except the unemployment rate, display time series properties consistent with a stationary process around a stochastic trend. Real GDP and real fixed capital formation are best represented by a random walk with drift. There is some evidence of a cyclical component in nominal

GDP. This appears to be generated by the behaviour of the price level.

- A VAR model of the UK economy permitted analysis of the source and impact of shocks. Broadly speaking, it was found that the main source of output variation is changes in real aggregate demand.
- There is little or no support for a political business cycle (PBC) of the type suggested by Nordhaus. However, the fiscal deficit displays behaviour consistent with political influence, and so does inflation, a result consistent with the observation of cycles in nominal GDP.
- There is no evidence of deterministic chaos for any of the series considered. However, there is some support for non-linearity in real and nominal GDP, prices and unemployment.

The implications of these findings, for both macroeconomic policy formulation and future research, will be considered in the concluding chapter.

6

Evaluation and Conclusions

6.1 Introduction

Given the purpose of this book, to consider recent theoretical advances in the analysis of business cycles and empirically to evaluate the resulting competing theories, in this chapter we draw together the various aspects of analysis covered, and provide an overall view of what is known about the business cycle and what needs to be done to enhance our knowledge of this phenomenon. In the next section we present an overview of the last four chapters. We then consider policy implications arising out of the theoretical analysis and empirical results. Finally, we use our overall evaluation to suggest avenues for further research.

6.2 An Overall Evaluation

This book has concentrated on three areas which have been the subject of recent work. First, the equilibrium approach to analysing business cycles received a considerable impetus in the early 1980s with the development of *real business cycle models*. While these concentrated on explaining cyclical activity as the result of the optimal intertemporal response of economic agents to productivity shocks, it is clear from later work that this is too restrictive an interpretation. Essentially, recent versions of the equilibrium approach emphasize the importance of real shocks, both demand and supply, and downgrade significantly the part played by nominal shocks, which had been such an important feature of the equilibrium *monetary business cycles* of the 1970s.

Second, the presence of non-linearities in macroeconomic time series is not inconsistent with the equilibrium approach but, if they do exist, a significant re-evaluation of how business cycles occur is required. The non-linearities may, of course, arise because of non-market clearing, but identifying the causes of non-linearities is more difficult. Testing for chaos, as well as non-linearities, has been the subject of recent work; but large data sets, which are not available for the key macroeconomic time series, are required for satisfactory testing.

Third, there has been a resurgence of interest in the influence of political decision-making on macroeconomic policy, particularly with regard to the effects that the electoral cycle and partisan politics have on policy. That economic policy and the political process are closely related seems, on casual observation, to be undisputable, and it is important to see whether or not this is borne out by more formal testing procedures.

We have taken each of these areas and subjected them to both theoretical and empirical scrutiny. In very broad terms, we have found that the bulk of evidence favours the equilibrium approach to business cycle analysis, although with political pressures apparently influencing policy decisions, and we are unable to reject entirely non-linear structures within macroeconomic time series. To some extent these results are complementary because, for example, EBC models are often linearized before they are solved: however, as is common in economic analysis, we are left with more questions than answers.

More specifically, for the UK, the evidence on unit root tests suggests that output and other key real variables (except for the unemployment rate) follow random walks (for some, with drift), a result consistent with the stochastic equilibrium approach. In addition, the VAR model estimates for the UK confirm that output is influenced only by real factors, specifically real aggregate demand, a result also consistent with Pareto optimal, market clearing behaviour, although it can equally arise with a Keynesian-type macroeconomic model. Note, however, that incorporating non-linearities might change these results qualitatively as well as quantitatively. Finally, testing for the effects of political factors also favours the equilibrium approach. There appears to be no impact of political factors on real economic activity, even though there is a clear effect on the nominal and fiscal policy variables, and on the rate of price inflation.

Despite this empirical support, our review of the theoretical basis for the equilibrium approach suggests that our conclusions should not be too emphatic. It is important to realize that our empirical work is only exploratory, and that the null and alternative hypotheses are not equilibrium and disequilibrium modelling strategies, respectively. We have not found evidence which specifically contradicts the equilibrium approach but, as we have pointed out, there are many aspects of aggregate economic behaviour (particularly in the labour market) which are at odds with the market clearing assumption. The major conclusion of our study is therefore that the equilibrium approach does have *some* validity. However, our empirical work for the UK supports other recent results in concluding that conventional macroeconomic models are deficient, but that what this means is that a new research programme should be developed in macroeconomics to make good the large gaps in understanding which exist. The final section of this chapter provides some suggestions as to what that research programme should include.

6.3 Policy Implications

Before turning to the issue of the where to go from here, we shall draw some implications for macroeconomic policy from our empirical analysis of UK data.

The evidence (particularly fiscal) that policy variables are influenced by political factors, but that these appear only to have impact on the nominal variables, presents a clear policy implication – that we should take policy out of the hands of politicians. This would mean imposing strict limits on budget deficits and possibly for monetary control to be handed to an independent (but accountable) central bank with clearly defined (non-conflicting) constitutional objectives.

Theoretical arguments about credibility and reputation are also supportive of this general prescription. If policy is seen to be conducted independently of the political process, and the objectives of the policy-marker are clearly defined, there should be no conflict between the policy and Pareto optimal solutions for economic agents. The time-inconsistency problem is eliminated. In addition, there are likely to be benefits in terms of reduced uncertainty about nominal variables. As we discuss in the next section, the real effects of this uncertainty are potentially significant and need to be investigated further. In fact, an argument which has been used for adopting simple policy rules (rather than discretionary or complex feedback rules) is that we know too little about the economy to make sensible policy prescriptions. This nihilistic view may be only a temporary phenomenon.

Recent UK policy decisions moved policy towards the position just advocated. In particular, the participation of sterling in the Exchange Rate Mechanism (ERM) of the European Monetary System, from October 1990, effectively linked UK monetary policy to that of the Bundesbank (the German central bank); an institution with an unrivalled reputation for inflation fighting and renowned for its independence from political influences. Tensions following German unification, however, raised some doubts over whether the Bundesbank will maintain this reputation and retain its independence (which is, of course, also threatened by the proposed European Monetary Union). Looking further ahead, moves toward full European Monetary Union are tied to limits on budget deficits, which are also consistent with our policy conclusions. The turmoil in the ERM in September 1992 and sterling's withdrawal from it have, however, moved UK monetary and fiscal policy back into the realm of discretion.

6.4 Suggestions for Future Research

The overview presented above makes it clear that our analysis has answered few questions, and raised considerably more. This leads us to propose some areas of current (and future) research which should enhance our understanding of the behaviour of the macroeconomy and thereby facilitate the formulation of effective policy prescriptions.

Persistence, sources of shocks and empirical testing

The equilibrium approach to business cycle modelling can be seen as a natural progression of the Frischian (1933) approach to dynamic modelling, in which inherently linear dynamics generates cycles from shocks which hit the economy. However, the evidence on non-linearities suggests that these may be important in explaining the time series behaviour of macroeconomic variables.

If such non-linearities are important, then tests for random walks are inappropriate and are giving the wrong message about the persistence of shocks required to replicate actual behaviour. Also, any attempt to identify the sources of shocks would be influenced by the failure to impose appropriate non-linear structures. There is a need for more general tests of linearity, as well as the existing conventional tests on the form of that linearity, when analysing time series behaviour. Such tests do exist (e.g., see Harvey, 1989), and need to be used more frequently in empirical analysis. It should be noted that linearization is also an important solution technique when simulating equilibrium business cycle models. Singleton (1988) shows that, as a result, additional distortions are introduced and this is clearly also a cause for concern.

There have been significant developments in non-linear modelling of business cycles since the late 1970s. Boldrin and Woodford (1990) provide a survey of non-linear equilibrium models capable of displaying endogenous fluctuations and chaos. They argue that previous non-linear endogenous cycle literature (reviewed in chapter 3) had been broadly Keynesian in motivation and lacked an adequate behavioural foundation. The literature they survey shows that endogenous fluctuations (either periodic or chaotic) can persist in rigorously formulated equilibrium models, in which agents optimize with perfect foresight, in the absence of exogenous shocks. It is thus possible to develop non-linear EBC models, such as that of Grandmont (1985), which differ from MBC or RBC models in that they do not rely on shocks of any sort as a source of energy. Shocks merely add to the irregularity of economic fluctuations.

In determining the sources of shocks to disturb the economy and generate simulations to approximate actual behaviour, it has been necessary for equilibrium theorists to introduce significant persistence. As discussed, linearization may make this necessary. Alternatively, the shocks may not be specified well enough. In other words, the models do not identify accurately enough which shocks are actually hitting the economy and, as a result, too much weight is being placed on the shocks that are included. One development which could prove fruitful would be introduce shock-generation models. For example, if technological shocks are important, then incorporating work on diffusion of innovations (such as Metcalfe, 1984), could considerably enrich the dynamic processes involved. More attention may also have to be paid to the effects of structural breaks (e.g., Solomou, 1987; Perron, 1989).

Trends and endogenous growth

Consideration of the diffusion of technology, and the explanation of how and why economies grow, leads naturally into a discussion of the endogeneity of technical progress. This has already been identified as a potentially fruitful area for further research (King et al., 1988b; Romer, 1989) and important developments are being made.

Two interesting implications of the endogeneity of growth may be noted. First, with regard to the source of shocks in the economy, productivity is no longer generated by an exogenous stochastic process. Second, production functions exhibit increasing returns to scale and consequently there is inherent non-linearity in the model.

The political process and EBC models

Another area in which significant progress has been made in the 1980s is in the application of game-theoretic models to the analysis of the role of the government and its interaction with the economy. This literature, which is discussed in chapter 4, assumes that the government has its own objective function, which is not necessarily a function of social welfare. It is related to the political business cycle literature (also reviewed in chapter 4), in that the government is interested in winning elections and, to do so, manipulates the economy.

Models of this type have been criticized for not allowing the electorate to respond to rising inflation (by increasing wage demands, for example) and for not broadening the game to include more than two players, the government and an homogeneous electorate. Similarly, RBC models rarely consider the role of the government and the heterogeneity of economic agents; although King et al. (1988b) have begun to address these issues. The game-theoretic literature suggests how this might be achieved, and it can clearly be generalized, although perhaps not without difficulty, to cover multiplayer games, with each group of players having a well defined objective function and sets of decision variables and strategies. The interaction between economic policy and political processes has considerable potential as an explanation of the behaviour of the macroeconomy.

The role of money and banking

It was argued in chapter 2 that the role of money and banking is inadequately considered in the RBC literature. However, in the 1970s and 1980s, interest in the role of the financial, and particularly the banking, system in business cycles has grown. Mullineux (1990, ch. 3) surveys some of the burgeoning literature on the financial instability hypothesis. Kindleberger (1978) undertakes an historical analysis of financial crises, and Minsky (1977, 1982a,b, 1986) provides a theoretical discussion. Kindleberger and Minsky emphasize irrational speculative finance as a feature of the upswing; and the role of uncertainty, which allows changes in 'animal spirits', brought about perhaps by adverse real or monetary shocks, in bringing on a financial crisis. It is also possible to generate speculative bubbles under the rational expectations hypothesis (Flood and Garber, 1982; Blanchard and Watson, 1986).

Sinai (1978, 1980) and Eckstein and Sinai (1986) emphasize the role of 'credit crunches', rather than financial crises, in business cycles. Credit crunches (or 'crumbles') may occur when banks reappraise risks and become less willing to lend, as in the US recession in the early 1990s. They develop into potential crises when the creditworthiness of banks is called into question by the rise in bad debts on their books, which causes them to become yet more cautious about lending. If deposits are withdrawn, the banks become not only unwilling but unable to maintain previous levels of lending, and experience liquidity problems – and possibly insolvency. A systemic crisis occurs when problems at individual banks raise question marks about the position of other banks, leading to widespread deposit withdrawals. Hence the banking system can play a crucial role in the generation and propagation of cycles within the economy, as the experience of the late 1980s and early 1990s shows.

Given that the major part of the money supply is created by banks, it is evident that closer attention needs to be paid to the money generation process in business cycle models. Rather than rely on monetary shocks, unwittingly or knowingly created by the government, the role of bank credit creation and the wider financial system in financing expansion and technological innovation should be carefully investigated. If the rate of technological innovation does depend on availability of finance, then real and monetary impulses should not be regarded as separable. It also becomes questionable whether the impulses are best modelled as shocks. A clearer understanding of technological innovation and the role of the financial system may allow their influences to be endogenized. Schumpeter (1934, 1935, 1939) and Shackle (1968) saw a linkage between technological innovation and the banking system's willingness to sponsor speculative ventures. Amendola and Gaffard (1988) have recently developed a model of endogenous technical change which attempts to take account of the availability of finance, and Bencivenga and Smith (1991) relate the endogenous growth rate to the provision of liquidity services by financial intermediaries.

The implications of uncertainty

Minsky's financial instability hypothesis assumes that economic decision-making takes place under uncertainty, rather than risk (Knight, 1921). The New Keynesian approach (surveyed in Greenwald and Stiglitz, 1988) also emphasizes risk and uncertainty. Hitherto, the resulting models have been essentially linear, but the research may eventually throw up key non-linearities. Alternatively, the main source of bifurcations, which are a feature of non-linear models and lead to qualitative changes in behaviour, could be shifts in expectations under uncertainty (Azariadis, 1981). The changes in expectations might, in turn, result naturally as the cycle evolves, or be precipitated by external shocks.

A further development, related to the idea of uncertainty and individuals' reaction to it, opens up a large range of potential future directions in macroeconomics. Blanchard and Mankiw (1988) have developed a framework for the analysis of consumption which moves beyond the basic premise of certainty equivalence. In their words, they wish to 'take uncertainty seriously'. In support of the Campbell and Mankiw hypothesis, Flacco and Parker (1990) have provided empirical evidence that income uncertainty is a significant determinant of consumption. Grinols and Turnovsky (1990) argue, more generally, that an understanding of the relationship between market uncertainties and economic performance is required. They see this in the context of explaining how the financial and real economies are linked. The impact of uncertainty (more correctly, risk, in the sense of Knight, 1921) is well understood in the analysis of financial markets, and has been the source of the main developments in the understanding of how they operate (e.g., portfolio selection (Markowitz, 1959) and capital market equilibrium (Sharpe, 1964)).

Developing a stochastic version of the Lucas (1982) cash-in-advance model, Svennson (1985) has discussed the impact of uncertainty in a general equilibrium macroeconomic framework, particularly with regard to the distinction between real and nominal interest rates. Stultz (1986) has examined the impact of monetary policy variability on interest rates. Grinols and Turnovsky (1990) generate a macroeconomic model with a well developed financial sector, and point out that the rational expectations equilibrium requires consistent specification of the first two moments of the endogenous variables. It is interesting to note that this makes the equilibrium solution non-linear. Furthermore, the solution that they construct involves both exogenously and endogenously determined risk. This observation is interesting in the context of our previous comments about the need for the sources and nature of shocks to be isolated, in order properly to explain the character of business cycles. There are clearly numerous potentially interesting variations on the general theme of uncertainty at a macroeconomic level, and such developments should improve our understanding of the cyclical behaviour of the aggregate economy.

One of the basic problems of the RBC approach is its reliance on special forms of the utility function to generate empirically meaningful results. Thus, Kydland and Prescott (1982) require the marginal utility of leisure to be determined by past leisure outcomes, while King and Rebelo (1988) demonstrate that the neoclassical growth model requires unrealistically high real interest rates to account for different patterns of economic growth between the US and Japan. A possible solution to this is to use the concept of non-expected utility, although this takes us out of the standard neoclassical paradigm. Work on non-expected utility has developed from the initial suggestion of Kreps and Porteus (1978) that it is sensible to separate out an individual's attitude towards risk and their behaviour towards intertemporal substitution. Crucially for RBC models, this allows preferences to be modelled for a representative agent with a low elasticity of intertemporal substitution and a low coefficient of relative risk aversion. At present, non-expected utility has been applied specifically to consumption (Weil, 1990) and portfolio choice (Svennson, 1989) and favourable empirical evidence has been offered by Bufman and Leiderman (1990).

Non-market clearing and RBC models

If the main contribution of equilibrium models is viewed as establishing the importance of real shocks and intertemporal choice to explain the behaviour of aggregate economic activity, there is a clear need to incorporate these ideas into models in which the concept of continuous market clearing is abandoned. There has been much debate about the relative merits of New Keynesian and RBC models of the macroeconomy. Greenwald and Stiglitz (1988) argue forcefully that the non-market clearing approach provides a better explanation of the source of cycles. They propose that the effects of asymmetric information on equity markets and labour markets are the key sources of market failure. Other approaches rely on the existence of long-term contracts which are optimal on risk-sharing grounds (Azariadis, 1975) and which can, in an overlapping framework (Taylor, 1979), provide a very comprehensive set of macrodynamics. The effect of costly price changes (e.g., Parkin, 1986) and the presence of efficiency wages (Akerlof and Yellen, 1985) also introduce nominal rigidity and non-market clearing solutions into models in which economic agents maximize an objective function, as in the equilibrium approach.

Such work is best seen as a natural response to the development of the equilibrium approach. The need to provide microfoundations for non-market clearing explanations of aggregate economic behaviour has increased our understanding of the behaviour of goods, labour and capital markets. There is clearly considerable benefit to be gained from attempting to combine the best of both approaches.

Bibliography

Abraham, K. G. and Katz, L. P. 1986: Cyclical unemployment: sectoral shifts or aggregate disturbances. *Journal of Political Economy*, 94, 507–22.

Adelman, I. 1960: Business cycles – endogenous or stochastic. *Economic Journal*, 70, 783–96.

Adelman, I. and Adelman, P. L. 1959: Dynamic properties of the Klein–Goldberger model. *Econometrica*, 27, 597–625.

Akerlof, G. A. and Stiglitz, J. E. 1969: Capital wages and structural unemployment. *Economic Journal*, 79, 269–81.

Akerlof, G. A. and Yellen, J. L. 1985: A near-rational model of the business cycle with wage and price inertia. *Quarterly Journal of Economics*, 100 (Suppl.), 823–38.

Akerman, J. 1947: Political economic cycles. *Kyklos*, 1, 107–17.

Alesina, A. 1987: Macroeconomic policy in a two-party system as a repeated game. *Quarterly Journal of Economics*, 102, 651–78.

Alesina, A. 1988: Macroeconomics and politics. *NBER Macroeconomics Annual*, 13–52.

Alesina, A. 1989: Politics and business cycles in industrial democracies. *Economic Policy*, no. 8, 57–98.

Alesina, A. and Cuckierman, A. 1987: The politics of ambiguity. Working paper 2468. Cambridge, Massachusetts: National Bureau of Economic Research.

Alesina, A. and Roubini, N. 1990: Political business cycle in OECD economies. NBER working paper no. 3478.

Alesina, A. and Sachs, J. 1988: Political parties and the business cycle in the United States, 1948–1984. *Journal of Money, Credit and Banking*, 20 (February), 63–82.

Alesina, A., Cohen, G. D. and Roubini, N. 1992: Macroeconomic policy and elections in OECD democracies. Centre for Economic Policy Research, discussion paper series no. 608.

Alt, J. 1979: *The Politics of Economic Decline.* Cambridge: Cambridge University Press.

Alt, J. E. and Chrystal, K. A. 1983: *Political Economy.* Berkeley, California: Berkeley University Press.

Ambler, S. and Phaneuf, L. 1988: Interest rate innovations and the business cycle. *Economics Letters,* 26, 305–9.

Amendola, M. and Gaffard, J.-L. 1988: *The Innovative Choice: an Economic Analysis of the Dynamics of Technology.* Oxford: Basil Blackwell.

Anderson, E. E. 1977: Further evidence of the Monte Carlo cycle in business activity. *Economic Inquiry,* 16, 269–76.

Anderson, T. M. 1989: Credibility of policy announcements. *European Economic Review,* 33, 13–30.

Attfield, C. L. P., Demery, D. and Duck, N. W. 1981: Unanticipated monetary growth, output and the price level: UK, 1946–77. *European Economic Review,* 16, 367–85.

Azariadis, C. 1975: Implicit contracts and underemployment equilibria. *Journal of Political Economy,* 83, 1183–202.

Azariadis, C. 1981: Self-fulfilling prophecies. *Journal of Economic Theory,* 25, 380–96.

Azariadis, C. and Guesnerie, R. 1986: Sunspots and cycles. *Review of Economic Studies,* 53, 725–38.

Backus, D. and Driffill, J. 1985a: Inflation and reputation. *American Economic Review,* 75, 530–38.

Backus, D. and Driffill, J. 1985b: Rational expectations and policy credibility following a change of regime. *Review of Economic Studies,* 52, 211–21.

Backus, D. K. and Kehoe, P. J. 1989: International evidence on the historical properties of business cycles. Federal Reserve Bank of Minneapolis, Research Department, working paper no. 402R.

Backus, D. K., Kehoe, P. J. and Kydland, P. E. 1990: International borrowing and world business cycles. Federal Reserve Bank of Minneapolis, Research Department, working paper no. 426R.

Balducci, R., Candella, G. and Ricci, G. 1984: A generalization of R. Goodwin's model with rational behaviour of economic agents. In Goodwin et al. (1984), op. cit.

Balke, N. S. 1991: Partisanship theory, macroeconomic outcome and endogenous elections. *Southern Economic Journal,* 57(4), 920–35.

Balke, N. S. and Fomby, T. B. 1991: Shifting trends, segmented trends and infrequent permanent shocks. *Journal of Monetary Economics,* 28, 61–85.

Barnett, W. A. and Hinich, M. 1990: Has chaos been discovered with economic data? Paper presented at the International Conference on Operations Research, Vienna, Austria, 28–31 August.

Barnett, W. A. and Ping Chen 1988: The aggregation-theoretical monetary aggregates are chaotic and have strange attractors: an econometric application of mathematical chaos. In W. A. Barnett, R. B. Ernst and W. Halbert (eds), *Dynamic Econometric Modelling*, Proceedings of the Third International Symposium in Economic Theory and Econometrics. Cambridge: Cambridge University Press.

Barro, R. J. 1976: Rational expectations and the role of monetary policy. *Journal of Monetary Economics*, 2, 1–32: reprinted in Barro (1981), op. cit.

Barro, R. J. 1977: Unanticipated money growth and unemployment in the United States. *American Economic Review*, 67 (March), 107–15.

Barro, R. J. 1978: Unanticipated money, output and the price level in the United States. *Journal of Political Economy*, 86, 549–80.

Barro, R. J. 1979: On the determination of public debt. *Journal of Political Economy*, 87, 940–71.

Barro, R. J. 1981: *Money Expectations and Business Cycles*. New York: Academic Press.

Barro, R. J. 1986: Comment. In *Macroeconomics Annual 1*, National Bureau of Economic Research. Cambridge, Massachusetts: MIT Press, 135–9.

Barro, R. J. 1989: *Modern Business Cycle Theory*. Cambridge, Massachusetts: Harvard University Press.

Barro, R. J. 1990: Government spending in a simple model of endogenous growth. *Journal of Political Economy*, 98, 103–35.

Barro, R. J. and Gordon, D. B. 1983a: A positive theory of monetary policy in a natural rate model. *Journal of Political Economy*, 91, 584–610.

Barro, R. J. and Gordon, D. B. 1983b: Rules, discretion and reputation in a model of monetary policy. *Journal of Monetary Economics*, 12, 101–25.

Barro, R. J. and Grossman, H. 1976: *Money, Employment and Inflation*. Cambridge: Cambridge University Press.

Barro, R. J. and Hercowitz, Z. 1980: Money stock revisions and unanticipated monetary growth. *Journal of Monetary Economics*, 6, 257–67.

Barro, R. J. and Rush, M. 1980: Unanticipated money and economic activity. In S. Fischer (ed.), *Rational Expectations and Economic Policy*. Chicago: University of Chicago Press.

Baumol, W. J. 1970: *Economic Dynamics: an Introduction*, 3rd edn. London: Macmillan.

Baumol, W. J. and Benhabid, J. 1989: Chaos: significance, mechanism, and economic applications. *Journal of Economic Perspectives*, 3(1), 77–106.

Bean, C. R. 1990: Endogenous growth and the procyclical behaviour of productivity. *European Economic Review*, 34, 355–63.

Beaudry, P. and Dinardo, J. 1991: The effects of implicit contracts on the movement of wages over the business cycle: evidence from micro data. *Journal of Political Economy*, 99, 665–88.

Beck, N. 1984: Domestic political sources of American monetary policy: 1955–82. *Journal of Politics*, XLVI, 786–815.

Begg, D. K. H. 1984: Rational expectations and bond pricing: modelling the term structure with and without certainty equivalence. *Economic Journal*, 94, 45–58.

Bencivenga, V. R. and Smith, B. D. 1991: Financial intermediation and endogenous growth. *Review of Economic Studies*, 58, 195–209.

Benhabib, J. and Day, R. H. 1981: Rational choice and erratic behaviour. *Review of Economic Studies*, 48, 459–72.

Benhabib, J. and Day, R. H. 1982: A characterization of erratic dynamics in the overlapping generating model. *Journal of Economic Dynamics and Control*, 4, 37–55.

Benhabib, J. and Nishimura, K. 1979: The Hopf bifurcation and the existence and stability of closed orbits in multisector models of optimal economic growth. *Journal of Economic Theory*, 35, 145–70.

Benhabib, J. and Nishimura, K. 1985: Competitive equilibrium cycles. *Journal of Economic Theory*, 45, 284–306.

Benhabib, J. and Nishimura, K. 1989: Stochastic equilibrium oscillations. *International Economic Review*, 30, 85–102.

Bernanke, B. S. 1986: Alternative explanations of the money–income correlation. *Carnegie–Rochester Conference Series on Public Policy*, 25, 49–100.

Bewley, T. 1986: Dynamic implications of the form of the budget constraint. In H. F. Sonneschein (ed.), *Models of Economic Dynamics*. New York: Springer-Verlag.

Black, P. 1982: General equilibrium and business cycles, National Bureau of Economic Research, working paper no. 950, August; reprinted in Black (1987), op. cit.

Black, P. 1987: *Business Cycles and Equilibrium*. Oxford: Basil Blackwell.

Blackburn, K. and Christensen, M. 1989: Monetary policy and policy credibility, theories and evidence. *Journal of Economic Literature*, 27 (March), 1–45.

Blackburn, K. and Ravn, M. O. 1990: Business cycles in the UK: facts and fictions. Working Paper, University of Southampton.

Blackburn, K. and Ravn, M. O. 1991: Contemporary macroeconomic fluctuations: an international perspective. Working Paper, University of Southampton.

Blanchard, O. J. 1986: Empirical structural evidence of wages, prices and employment in the US. Working paper no. 2044. Cambridge, Massachusetts: National Bureau for Economic Research.

Blanchard, O. J. 1989: A traditional interpretation of macroeconomic fluctuations. *American Economic Review*, 79, 1146–64.

Blanchard, O. J. and Mankiw, N. G. 1988: Consumption: beyond certainty equivalence. *American Economic Review*, 78 (papers and proceedings), 173–7.

Blanchard, O. J. and Quah, D. 1989: The dynamic effects of aggregate demand and supply disturbances. *American Economic Review*, 79, 1146–64.

Blanchard, O. J. and Watson, M. W. 1982: Bubbles, rational expectations and financial markets. In P. Wachtel (ed.), *Crises in the Economic and Financial Structure*. Lexington, Massachusetts: Lexington Books; ch. 11, 295–316.

Blanchard, O. J. and Watson, M. W. 1986: Are business cycles all alike? In R. J. Gordon (ed.), *The American Business Cycle*. Chicago: University of Chicago Press.

Blatt, J. M. 1978: On the econometric approach to business cycle modelling. *Oxford Economic Papers*, 30(2), 292–300.

Blatt, J. M. 1980: On the Frisch model of business cycles. *Oxford Economic Papers*, 32(3), 476–9.

Blatt, J. M. 1983: *Dynamic Economic Systems*. Armouk, New York: M. G. Sharpe.

Blinder, A. S. and Fischer, S. 1981: Inventories, rational expectations and the business cycle. *Journal of Monetary Economics*, 8, 277–304.

Blinder, A. S. and Maccini, L. J. 1991: Taking stock: a critical assessment of recent research in invention. *Journal of Economic Perspectives*, 5(1), 73–96.

Boddy, R. and Crotty, J. 1975: Class conflict and macro-policy: the political business cycle. *Review of Radical Political Economics*, 7, 1–19.

Boldrin, M. 1986: Paths of optimal accumulation in two-sector models. In W. Barnett, J. Geweke and K. Shell (eds), *Economic Complexity: Chaos, Sunspots, Bubbles and Nonlinearity*. Cambridge: Cambridge University Press.

Boldrin, M. and Woodford, M. 1990: Equilibrium models displaying endogenous fluctuations and chaos: a survey. *Journal of Monetary Economics*, 25, 189–222.

Boschen, J. and Grossman, H. I. 1982: Tests of equilibrium macroeconomics using contemporaneous monetary data. *Journal of Monetary Economics*, 10, 309–34.

Boschen, J. P. and Mills, L. O. 1988: Tests of the relation between money and output in the real business cycle model. *Journal of Monetary Economics*, 22, 355–74.

Brock, W. A. 1986: Distinguishing random and deterministic systems: abridged version. *Journal of Economic Theory*, 40, 168–95.

Brock, W. and Dechert, W. D. 1988: Theorems on distinguishing deterministic and random systems. In W. Barnett, E. Berndt and H. White (eds), *Dynamic Econometric Modelling, Proceedings of the Third International Symposium in Economic Theory and Econometrics*. Cambridge: Cambridge University Press.

Brock, W. A. and Sayers, C. L. 1988: Is the business cycle characterised by deterministic chaos? *Journal of Monetary Economics*, 22, 71–90.

Brock, W. A., Dechert, W. D. and Scheinkman, J. 1987: A test for independence based upon the correlation dimension. Manuscript, Madison: University of Wisconsin.

Bronfenbrenner, M. 1969: *Is the Business Cycle Obsolete?* New York: John Wiley.

Bufman, G. and Leiderman, L. 1990: Consumption and asset returns under non-expected utility. *Economics Letters*, 34, 231–5.

Butler, A. 1990: A methodological approach to chaos: are economists missing the point? *Federal Reserve Bank of St. Louis Review*, 72(2), 36–48.

Campbell, J. Y. and Mankiw, N. W. 1987a: Permanent and transitory components in macroeconomic fluctuations. *American Economic Review*, 77, 111–17.

Campbell, J. Y. and Mankiw, N. W. 1987b: Are output fluctuations transitory? *Quarterly Journal of Economics*, 102, 857–80.

Campbell, J. Y. and Mankiw, N. W. 1989: International evidence on the persistence of economic fluctuations. *Journal of Monetary Economics*, 23, 319–33.

Cantor, R. and Mark, N. C. 1988: The international transmission of real business cycles. *International Economic Review*, 29, 493–507.

Canzoneri, M. O. 1985: Monetary policy games and the role of private information. *American Economic Review*, 75(5), 1056–70.

Chan, L. K. C. 1988: Unanticipated monetary policy and real economic activity: some cross-regime evidence. *Journal of Monetary Economics*, 22, 439–59.

Chang, W. W. and Smyth, D. J. 1970: The existence and persistence of cycles in a nonlinear model: Kaldor's 1940 model re-examined. *Review of Economic Studies*, 38(113), 37–44.

Chappel, H. W., Jr and Keech, W. R. 1988: The unemployment rate consequences of partisan monetary policies. *Southern Economic Journal*, 55, 107–22.

Chappell, D. and Peel, D. A. 1979: On the political theory of the business cycle. *Economics Letters*, 2, 327–32.

Chen, P. 1988: Empirical and theoretical evidence of economic chaos. *System Dynamics Review*, 4, 81–108.

Chiang, A. C. 1974: *Fundamental Methods of Mathematical Economics*, (2nd edn). Tokyo: McGraw-Hill Kogakusha.

Chiarella, C. 1986: Perfect foresight models and the dynamic instability problem from a higher viewpoint. *Economic Modelling*, 3, 283–92.

Christiano, L. J. and Ljungquist, L. 1988: Money does Granger-cause output in the bivariate money output relation. *Journal of Monetary Economics*, 22, 217–35.

Chrystal, K. A. and Dowd, K. 1989: Disaggregate supply: evidence for the UK. *Applied Economics*, 21, 1397–409.

Clarke, P. K. 1989: Trend revision in real output and unemployment. *Journal of Econometrics*, 40, 15–32.

Cochrane, J. H. 1988: How big is the random walk in GNP? *Journal of Political Economy*, 96, 893–920.

Cochrane, J. H. 1991: A critique of the application of unit root tests. *Journal of Economic Dynamics and Control*, 15, 275–84.

Cooley, T. P. and Hansen, G. D. 1989: The inflation tax in a real business cycle model. *American Economic Review*, 79, 733–48.

Cooper, R. and Haltiwanger, J. 1990: Inventories and the propagation of sectoral shocks. *American Economic Review*, 80, 170–90.

Cuckierman, A. 1986: Central bank behaviour and credibility: some recent theoretical developments. *Federal Reserve Bank of St. Louis Review*, 68, 5–17.

Cuckierman, A. and Meltzer, A. H. 1986a: A positive theory of discretionary policy, the cost of a democratic government, and the benefits of a constitution. *Economic Inquiry*, 24 (July), 367–88.

Cuckierman, A. and Meltzer, A. H. 1986b: A theory of ambiguity, credibility and inflation under discretion, and asymmetric information. *Econometrica*, 53 (September), 1099–128.

Cugno, F. and Montrucchio, L. 1984: Some new techniques for modelling nonlinear economic fluctuations: a brief survey. In Goodwin et al. (1984), op. cit., 146–65.

Davis, S. J. 1987: Fluctuations in the pace of labour reallocation. *Carnegie–Rochester Conference Series on Public Policy*, 27, 335–402.

Day, R. H. 1982: Irregular growth cycles. *American Economic Review*, 72(3), 406–14.

Day, R. H. 1983: The emergence of chaos from classical economic growth. *Quarterly Journal of Economics*, 98, 201–13.

Day, R. H. and Lin, T. Y. 1992: A Keynesian business cycle. In E. J. Nell and W. Semmler (eds), *Nicolas Kaldor and Mainstream Economics*. London: Macmillan.

Day, R. H. and Shafer, J. W. 1985: Keynesian chaos. *Journal of Macroeconomics*, 7, 277–95.

Day, R. H. and Shafer, J. W. 1987: Ergodic fluctuations in deterministic economic models. *Journal of Economic Behaviour and Organization*, 8, 339–61.

De Long, J. B. and Summers, L. H. 1986: Are business cycles symmetrical? In R. J. Gordon (ed.), *The American Business Cycle*. Chicago: University of Chicago Press.

Desai, M. 1973: Growth cycles and inflation in a model of class struggle. *Journal of Economic Theory*, 6, 527–45.

Desai, M. and Shah, A. 1981: Growth cycles and induced technical change. *Econometrica*, 91, 1006–10.

Di Matteo, M. 1984: Alternative monetary policies in a classical business cycle. In Goodwin et al. (1984), op. cit., 14–24.

Dickinson, D. G., Driscoll, M. J. and Ford, J. L. 1982: Rational expectations, random parameters and the non-neutrality of money. *Economica*, 49, 241–8.

Dolado, J. T., Jenkinson, T. and Sosvilla-Rivero, S. 1990: Cointegration and unit roots. *Journal of Economic Surveys*, 4, 249–73.

Dornbusch, R. 1976: Expectations and exchange rate dynamics. *Journal of Political Economy*, 84, 1161–76.

Dotsey, M. 1990: The economic effects of production taxes in a stochastic growth model. *American Economic Review*, 80, 1168–82.

Downs, A. 1957: *The Economic Theory of Democracy*. New York: Harper.

Duesenberry, J. 1949: *Income, Saving and the Theory of Consumer Behaviour*. Cambridge, Massachusetts: Harvard University Press.

Durlauf, S. N. 1989: Output persistence, economic structure, and the choice of stabilisation policy. *Brookings Papers on Economic Activity*, 2, 69–116.

Eckstein, A. and Sinai, A. 1986: The mechanisms of the business cycle in the postwar era. In R. J. Gordon (ed.), *The American Business Cycle*. Chicago: University of Chicago Press.

Eichenbaum, M. 1991: Real business cycle theory: wisdom or whimsy? *Journal of Economic Dynamics and Control*, 15, 607–26.

Eichenbaum, M. and Singleton, K. J. 1986: Do equilibrium real business cycle theories explain postwar US business cycles? In *Macroeconomics Annual*. Cambridge, Massachusetts: MIT Press, 91–146.

Ellis, C. J. 1989: An equilibrium politico-economic model. *Economic Inquiry*, XXVII, 521–8.

Ellis, C. J. 1991: Endogenous voting in a partisan model with rational voters. *Journal of Macroeconomics*, 13, 267–78.

Englander, A. S. 1991: Optional monetary policy design: rules versus discretion again. *Federal Reserve Bank of New York Quarterly Review*, 15, no. 3–4, Winter, 65–79.

Engle, R. 1982: Autoregressive conditional heteroscedasticity with estimates of the variance of UK inflation. *Econometrica*, 50, 987–1007.

Engle, R. F. and Granger, C. W. J. 1987: Cointegration and error correction: representation, estimation and testing. *Econometrica*, 55(2), 251–76.

Engle, R. P. and Watson, M. W. 1981: A one factor time series model of metropolitan wage rates. *Journal of the American Statistical Association*, 76, 774–80.

Falk, B. 1986: Further evidence on the asymmetric behaviour of economic time series over the business cycle. *Journal of Political Economy*, 94, 1096–109.

Feiwel, G. R. 1974: Reflection on Kalecki's theory of the political business cycle. *Kyklos*, 27, 21–48.

Fels, R. 1964: Summary of Schumpeter's theory of the business cycle. In J. A. Schumpeter, *Business Cycles: a Theoretical, Historical and Statistical Analysis of the Capitalist Process*, abridged edn. New York: McGraw-Hill, 424–41.

Fisher, I. 1925: Our unstable dollar and the so-called business cycle. *Journal of the American Statistical Association*, 20(149), 179–202.

Flacco, P. R. and Parker, R. E. 1990: Some evidence on the influence of income uncertainty on aggregate consumption. *Journal of Macroeconomics*, 12, 653–62.

Flood, R. P. and Garber, P. M. 1982: Bubbles, runs and gold monetization. In P. L. Wachtel (ed.), *Crises in the Economic and Financial Structure*. Lexington, Massachusetts: Lexington Books; ch. 10, 275–94.

Ford, J. L. and Peng, W. S. 1993: Expectations, investment, the business cycle and economic development in the work of G. L. S. Shackle. Discussion paper, University of Birmingham; *Review of Political Economy*, 5(2), forthcoming.

Frank, M. Z. and Stengos, T. 1988a: Chaotic dynamics in economic time series. *Journal of Economic Surveys*, 2, 103–33.

Frank, M. Z. and Stengos, T. 1988b: Some evidence concerning macroeconomic chaos. *Journal of Monetary Economics*, 22, 423–38.

Frey, B. S. 1978: *Modern Political Economy*. Oxford: Martin Robertson.

Frey, B. S. and Schneider, F. 1978a: A political economic model of the UK. *Economic Journal*, 88, 243–53.

Frey, B. S. and Schneider, F. 1978b: An empirical study of politico-economic interaction in the U.S. *Review of Economics and Statistics*, LX(2), 174–83.

Frey, B. S. and Schneider, F. 1979: An econometric model with an endogenous government sector. *Public Choice*, 34(1), 29–43.

Frey, B. S. and Schneider, F. 1988: Central Bank behaviour: a positive empirical analysis. *Journal of Monetary Economics*, 17, 291–315.

Friedlaender, A. F. 1973: Macro policy goals in the postwar period: a study in revealed preference. *Quarterly Journal of Economics*, 87, 25–43.

Friedman, M. 1957: *A Theory of the Consumption Function.* National Bureau of Economic Research General Series no. 63. Princeton: Princeton University Press.

Friedman, M. and Schwartz, A. J. 1963: *A Monetary History of the United States: 1867–1960.* Princeton, New Jersey: Princeton University Press.

Friedman, M. and Schwartz, A. J. 1982: *Monetary Trends in the US and the UK: 1867–1975.* Chicago, University of Chicago Press.

Frisch, R. 1933: Propagation and impulse problems in dynamic economics. In *Essays in Honour of Gustav Cassel.* London: George Allen and Unwin.

Froyen, R. T. and Waud, R. N. 1988: Real business cycles and the Lucas paradigm. *Economic Inquiry*, 26, 183–201.

Gabisch, G. 1984: Nonlinear models of business cycle theory. In G. Hammer and D. Pallaschke (ed.), *Selected Topics in Operations Research and Mathematical Economics.* Lecture Notes in Economics and Mathematical Systems 226. Berlin: Springer-Verlag, 205–22.

Gabisch, G. 1987: Nonlinearities in dynamic economic systems. *Atlantic Journal of Economics*, 15(4), 22–31.

Gabisch, G. and Lorenz, H. W. 1987: *Business Cycle Theory.* Lecture Notes in Economics and Mathematical Systems 283. Berlin: Springer-Verlag.

Gandolfo, G. 1980: *Economic Dynamics, Methods and Models*, Amsterdam: North Holland.

Garber, P. M. and King, R. G. 1983: Deep structural excavation? A critique of Euler equation methods. National Bureau of Economic Research, NBER technical working paper no. 31.

Gaynon, J. E. 1988: Short-run models and long-run forecasts: a note on the permanence of output fluctuations. *Quarterly Journal of Economics*, 103, 415–24.

George, D. A. R. 1981: Equilibrium and catastrophes in economics. *Scottish Journal of Political Economy*, 28, 43–61.

George, D. A. R. 1988: *Mathematical Modelling for Economists.* London: Macmillan.

George, D. A. R. and Oxley, L. T. 1985: Structural stability and model design. *Economic Modelling*, 2, 307–16.

George, D. A. R. and Oxley, L. T. 1991: Fixed money growth rules and the rate of inflation. *Scottish Journal of Political Economy*, 38, 209–26.

Glombowski, J. and Kruger, M. 1984: Unemployment insurance and cyclical growth. In Goodwin et al. (1984), op. cit. 25–46.

Goodwin, R. M. 1951: The nonlinear accelerator and the persistence of business cycles. *Econometrica*, 19(1), 1–17.

Goodwin, R. M. 1955: A model of cyclical growth. In E. Lundberg (ed.), *The Business Cycle in the Postwar World*. London: Macmillan.

Goodwin, R. M. 1967: A growth cycle. In C. H. Feinstein (ed.), *Socialism, Capitalism and Economic Growth*. Cambridge: Cambridge University Press, 54–8. Reprinted in E. K. Hunt and J. G. Schwartz (ed.) 1972: *A Critique of Economic Theory*. Harmondsworth (UK): Penguin Books; also in R. M. Goodwin, 1982: *Essays in Economic Dynamics*. London: Macmillan.

Goodwin, R. M. 1987: In R. M. Goodwin and L. F. Punzo, *The Dynamics of a Capitalist Economy*. Oxford: Basil Blackwell with Polity Press, chs 1–4.

Goodwin, R. M. 1990: *Chaotic Economic Dynamics*. Oxford: Clarendon Press.

Goodwin, R. M. 1991: Schumpeter, Keynes and the theory of economic evolution. *Journal of Evolutionary Economics*, 1(1), 29–47.

Goodwin, R. M., Kruger, M. and Vercelli, A. (ed.) 1984: *Nonlinear Models of Fluctuating Growth, An International Symposium, Siena, Italy, 24–27 March 1983*. Lecture Notes in Economic and Mathematical Systems 228. Berlin and New York: Springer-Verlag.

Gordon, R. J. 1982: Price inertia and policy ineffectiveness in the United States, 1890–1980. *Journal of Political Economy*, 90, 1087–1117.

Gordon, R. J. (ed.) 1986: *The American Business Cycle*. Chicago: University of Chicago Press.

Grandmont, J. M. 1985: On endogenous competitive cycles. *Econometrica*, 53, 995–1045.

Grandmont, J. M. 1986: Stabilising competitive cycles. *Journal of Economic Theory*, 40, 57–76.

Grandmont, J. M. and Laroque, G. 1986: Stability of cycles and expectations. *Journal of Economic Theory*, 40, 138–51.

Granger, C. W. J. and Newbold, P. 1986: *Forecasting Economic Time Series*. New York and London: Academic Press.

Grassberger, P. and Procaccia, I. 1983a: Measuring the strangeness of strange attractors. *Physics*, 90, 189–208.

Grassberger, P. and Procaccia, I. 1983b: Characterisation of strange attractors. *Physical Review Letters*, 50, 346–9.

Greenwald, B. and Stiglitz, J. E. 1987: Keynesian, New Keynesian and New Classical Economics. *Oxford Economic Papers*, 39, 119–32.

Greenwald, B. C. and Stiglitz, J. E. 1988: Examining alternative economic theories. *Brooking Papers on Economic Activity*, 1, 207–60.

Greenwood, J. and Huffman, G. N. 1991: Tax analysis in a real business cycle model. *Journal of Monetary Economics*, 27, 167–90.

Greenwood, J., Hercowitz, Z. and Huffman, G. W. 1988: Investment, capital utilization and the real business cycle. *American Economic Review*, 78, 402–17.

Grier, K. B. 1987: Presidential elections and Federal Reserve policy: an empirical test. *Southern Economic Journal*, 54, 475–86.

Grinols, E. L. and Turnovsky, S. J. 1990: Extrinsic risk, financial market volatility and macroeconomic performance. University of Illinois (Urbana–Champaign), working paper, April.

Grossman, S. J. and Weiss, L. 1982: Heterogeneous information and the theory of the business cycle. *Journal of Political Economy*, 90, 699–727.

Grossman, S. J., Hart, O. D. and Maskin, E. S. 1983: Unemployment with observable aggregate shocks. *Journal of Political Economy*, 91, 907–27.

Haberler, G. 1946: *Prosperity and Depression*. New York: United Nations.

Hall, R. E. 1978: Stochastic implications of the life cycle permanent income hypothesis: theory and evidence. *Journal of Political Economy*, 86, 971–88.

Haltiwanger, J. L. and Maccini, L. J. 1988: A model of inventory and layoff behaviour under uncertainty. *Economic Journal*, 98 (September), 731–45.

Hamilton, J. D. 1985: Uncovering financial market expectations of inflation. *Journal of Political Economy*, 93, 1224–41.

Hansen, A. H. 1957: *Business Cycles and National Income*. New York: Norton.

Hansen, G. 1985: Indivisible labour and the business cycle. *Journal of Monetary Economics*, 16, 309–27.

Harrod, R. F. 1948: *Towards a Dynamic Economics*. London: Macmillan.

Harvey, A. C. 1981: *Time Series Models*. Oxford: Philip Allan.

Harvey, A. C. 1989: *Forecasting Structural Time Series Models and the Kalman Filter*, Cambridge UK: Cambridge University Press.

Harvey, A. C. 1990: *The Econometric Analysis of Time Series*. Oxford: Philip Allan.

Havrilinsky, T. M. 1987: A partisanship theory of fiscal and monetary regimes. *Journal of Money, Credit and Banking*, August, 308–25.

Hayek, P. A. 1933: *Monetary Theory and the Trade Cycle*. London: Jonathan Cape.

Haynes, S. E. and Stone, J. A. 1990: Political models of the business cycle should be revived. *Economic Inquiry*, 78(3), 442–65.

Henon, M. 1976: A two-dimensional mapping with a strange attractor. *Communications in Mathematical Physics*, 50, 69–77.

Hibbs, D. A. 1977: Political parties and macroeconomic policy. *American Political Science Review*, 71, 1467–87.

Hibbs, D. A. 1987: *The American Political Economy*. Cambridge, Massachusetts: Harvard University Press.

Hickman, B. G. (ed.) 1972: *Econometric Models of Cyclical Behaviour*, 1 and 2. New York: Columbia University Press.

Hicks, J. R. 1949: Mr. Harrod's dynamic theory. *Economica*, XVI, 106–21.

Hicks, J. R. 1950: *A Contribution to the Theory of the Trade Cycle*. Oxford: Oxford University Press.

Hinich, M. 1982: Testing for Gaussianity and linearity of a stationary time series. *Journal of Time Series Analysis*, 3, 169–76.

Hinich, M. and Patterson, D. M. 1985: Evidence of nonlinearity in daily stock returns. *Journal of Business and Economics Statistics*, 3, 69–77.

Hotelling, H. 1929: Stability in competition. *Economic Journal*, 39, 41–57.

Hylleberg, S., Engle, R. F., Granger, C. W. J. and Yoo, B. S. 1990: Seasonal integration and cointegration. *Journal of Econometrics*, 44, 215–38.

Ichimura, S. 1954: Towards a general macroeconomic theory of fluctuations. In K. Kurihara (ed.), *Post Keynesian Economics*. New Brunswick, New Jersey: Rutgers University Press, ch. 8.

Jevons, W. S. 1884: *Investigations in Currency and Finance*. London: Macmillan.

Kaldor, N. 1940: A model of the trade cycle. *Economic Journal*, 50, 78–92; reprinted in Kaldor, N. 1980: *Essays on Economic Stability and Growth*. London: Duckworth.

Kaldor, N. 1954: The relationship of economic growth and cyclical fluctuations. *Economic Journal*, 54, 53–71.

Kaldor, N. 1957: A model of economic growth. *Economic Journal*, 67, 591–624.

Kalecki, M. 1943: Political aspects of full employment. *Political Quarterly*, 14, 322–30.

Keil, M. W. 1988: Is the business cycle really dead? *Southern Economic Journal*, 55, 86–99.

Kelsey, D. 1988: The economics of chaos or the chaos of economics. *Oxford Economic Papers*, 40(1), 1–31.

Kettl, D. F. 1986: *Leadership at the Fed*. New Haven: Yale University Press.

Keynes, J. M. 1936: *The General Theory of Employment, Interest and Money*. London: Macmillan.

Kim, K. and Schmidt, P. 1990: Some evidence on the accuracy of Phillips–Perron tests using alternative estimates of the nuisance parameters, *Economics Letters*, 34, 345–50.

Kindleberger, C. P. 1978: *Manias, Panics and Crashes*. New York: Basic Books.

King, R. G. 1981: Monetary information and monetary neutrality. *Journal of Monetary Economics*, 7, 195–206.

King, R. G. and Plosser, C. I. 1984: Money, credit and prices in a real business cycle economy. *American Economic Review*, 74, 363–80.

King, R. G. and Rebelo, S. T. 1988: Business cycles and endogenous growth. University of Rochester working paper.

King, R. G. and Rebelo, S. T. 1989: Transitional dynamics and economic growth in the neoclassical model. National Bureau of Economic Research, working paper no. 3185, November.

King, R. G., Plosser, C. I. and Rebelo, S. T. 1988a: Production, growth and business cycles I. The basic neoclassical model. *Journal of Monetary Economics*, 21, 195–232.

King, R. G., Plosser, C. I. and Rebelo, S. T. 1988b: Production, growth and business cycles II. New directions. *Journal of Monetary Economics*, 21, 309–41.

King, R. G., Plosser, C. I., Stock, J. H. and Watson, M. N. 1987: Stochastic trends and economic fluctuations. NBER discussion paper no. 2229.

King, R. G., Plosser C. I., Stock J. H. and Watson, M. W. 1991: Stochastic trends and economic fluctuations. *American Economic Review*, 81, 819–40.

Klein, L. R. and Preston, R. S. 1969: Stochastic nonlinear models. *Econometrica*, 37(1), 95–106.

Knight, P. H. 1921: *Risk Uncertainty and Profit*, new edn, 1971. Chicago: University of Chicago Press.

Koopmans, T. C. 1947: Measurement without theory. *Review of Economics and Statistics*, 29, 161–72.

Kormendi, R. C. and Meguire, P. G. 1984: Cross-regime evidence of macroeconomic rationality. *Journal of Political Economy*, 92, 875–908.

Kosobud, R. F. and O'Neill, W. D. 1972: Stochastic implications of orbital asymptotic stability of a nonlinear trade cycle model. *Econometrica*, 40(1), 69–86.

Kreps, D. and Porteus, E. 1978: Temporal resolution of uncertainty and dynamic choice theory. *Econometrica*, 46, 185–200.

Kretzmer, P. E. 1989: The cross-industry effects of unanticipated money in an equilibrium business cycle model. *Journal of Monetary Economics*, 23, 275–96.

Krol, R. and Ohonian, L. E. 1990: The impact of stochastic and deterministic trends and money-output causality. *Journal of Econometrics*, 45, 291–308.

Kunst, R. and Neusser, K. 1990: Cointegration in a macroeconomic system. *Journal of Applied Econometrics*, 5, 357–65.

Kurths, J. and Herzel, H. 1987: An attractor in a solar time series. *Physica*, 25D, 165–72.

Kydland, F. E. 1984: Labour force heterogeneity and the business cycle. *Carnegie–Rochester Conference Series on Public Policy*, 21, 173–208.

Kydland, F. E. and Prescott, E. C. 1977: Rules rather than discretion: inconsistency of optimal plans. *Journal of Political Economy*, 85, 473–92.

Kydland, F. E. and Prescott, E. C. 1982: Time to build and aggregate fluctuations. *Econometrica*, 50, 1345–70.

Kydland, F. E. and Prescott, E. C. 1988: The workweek of capital and its cyclical implications. *Journal of Monetary Economics*, 21, 343–60.

Lachler, U. 1982: On political business cycles with endogenous election dates. *Journal of Public Economics*, 17, 111–17.

Leijonhufvud, A. 1973: Effective demand failures. *Swedish Journal of Economics*, 75, 27–48.

Lillien, D. M. 1982: Sectoral shifts and cyclical unemployment. *Journal of Political Economy*, 90, 777–93.

Lindbeck, A. 1976: Stabilization policy in open economies with endogenous politicians. *American Economic Review, Papers and Proceedings*, 66, 1–19.

Lines, M. 1990: Slutsky and Lucas: random causes of the business cycle. *Structural Change and Economic Dynamics*, 1(2), 359–70.

Litterman, R. B. and Weiss, L. 1985: Money, real interest rates, and output: a reinterpretation of postwar US data. *Econometrica*, 53, 129–56.

Long, J. B. and Plosser, C. I. 1983: Real business cycles. *Journal of Political Economy*, 91, 39–69.

Long, J. B. and Plosser, C. I. 1987: Sectoral vs aggregate shocks in the business cycle. *American Economic Review*, 77, 333–7.

Lorenz, H. W. 1987: Strange attractors in multisector business cycle models. *Journal of Economic Behaviour and Organisation*, 8(3), 397–411.

Lorenz, H. W. 1989: *Nonlinear Dynamical Economics and Chaotical Motions*. Lecture Notes in Economics and Mathematical Systems 334. Berlin and New York: Springer-Verlag.

Lotka, A. J. 1956: *Elements of Mathematical Biology*. New York and London: Constable.

Lucas, R. E. Jr. 1972: Expectations and the neutrality of money. *Journal of Economic Theory*, 4, 103–24.

Lucas, R. E. Jr. 1975: An equilibrium model of the business cycle. *Journal of Political Economy*, 83, 1113–44.

Lucas, R. E. Jr. 1976: Econometric evaluation: a critique. In K. Brunner and A. H. Meltzer (eds), *The Phillips Curve and Labour Markets*.

Carnegie, Rochester Conference Series on Public Policy, 1. Amsterdam and New York: North-Holland.

Lucas, R. E. Jr. 1977: Understanding business cycles. In K. Brunner and A. H. Meltzer (eds), *Stabilisation of the Domestic and International Economy*. Carnegie–Rochester Conference Series on Public Policy 5, Amsterdam and New York: North Holland.

Lucas, R. E. Jr. 1982: Interest rates and currency prices in a two-country world. *Journal of Monetary Economics*, 10, 335–60.

Lucas, R. E. Jr. 1987: *Models of Business Cycles*. Yrjo Jahnsson Lectures. Oxford: Basil Blackwell/Oxford University Press.

Lucas, R. E. Jr. 1988: On the mechanics of economic development. *Journal of Monetary Economics*, 22, 3–42.

Lucas, R. E. Jr. and Stokey, N. L. 1983: Optimal fiscal and monetary policy in an economy without capital. *Journal of Monetary Economics*, 12, 55–93.

Lucas, R. E. Jr. and Stokey, N. L. 1984: Money and interest in a cash in advance economy. CMSEMS discussion paper no. 628, Northwestern University.

Luckett, D. G. and Potts, G. T. 1980: Monetary policy and partisan policies. *Journal of Money, Credit and Banking*, 12(3), 540–6.

MacRae, D. 1977: A political model of the business cycle. *Journal of Political Economy*, 85, 239–63.

Magill, M. S. P. 1979: The origins of cyclical motions in dynamic economic models. *Journal of Economic Dynamics and Control*, 1, 199–218.

Malliaris, A. G. and Urrutia, J. L. 1990: How big are the random walks in macroeconomic time series? Variance ratio tests. *Economics Letters*, 34, 113–16.

Mankiw, N. G., Romer, D. and Weil, N. D. 1990: A contribution to the empirics of economic growth. Discussion paper no. 1532. Harvard Institution of Economic Research, Harvard University, Cambridge, Massachusetts.

Markowitz, H. M. 1959: *Portfolio Selection*. Yale: Cowles Foundation. New Edition published 1991, Oxford: Basil Blackwell.

Marx, K. 1867: *Das Kapital*, vol. I; see also vols II (1885) and III (1894). London: Lawrence and Wishart.

Mathews, R. C. O. 1959: A note on crawling along the ceiling. *Review of Economic Studying*, 57(72), 10–15.

May, A. M. 1987: The political business cycle, an institutional critique and reconstruction. *Journal of Economic Issues*, XXI, 713–22.

McCallum, B. 1978: The political business cycle, an empirical test. *Southern Economic Journal*, XLIV, 504–15.

McCallum, B. T. 1983: A reconsideration of Sims' evidence concerning monetarism. *Economics Letters*, 13, 167–71.

McCallum, B. T. 1986: On real and sticky-price theories of the business cycle. *Journal of Money, Credit and Banking* 18(4), 397–414.

McCallum, B. T. 1989: Real business cycles. In R. J. Barro (1989), op. cit.

McCulloch, J. H. 1975: The Monte-Carlo cycle in business activity. *Economic Inquiry*, 13, 303–21.

Mendoza, E. G. 1991: Real business cycles in a small open economy. *American Economic Review*, 81(4), 797–818.

Merrick, J. J. Jr. 1983: Financial market efficiency, the decomposition of anticipated versus unanticipated monetary growth, and further tests of the relation between money and real output. *Journal of Money, Credit and Banking*, 15, 222–32.

Metcalfe, J. S. 1984: Impulse and diffusion in the study of technical change. In C. Freeman (ed.), *Long Waves in the World*. London: Francis Pinter, ch. 8.

Mezler, L. A. 1941: The nature and stability of inventory cycles. *Review of Economics and Statistics*, 23, 113–29.

Mills, T. 1991a: Nonlinear time series models in economics. *Journal of Economic Surveys*, 5, 215–42.

Mills, T. 1991b: Are fluctuations in UK output transitory or permanent? *The Manchester School*, LIX(1), 1–11.

Mills, T. and Taylor, M. P. 1989: Random walk components in output and exchange rates: some robust tests on UK data. *Bulletin of Economic Research*, 41(2), 215–42.

Minford, P. and Peel, D. 1982: The political theory of the business cycle. *European Economic Review*, 17, 253–70.

Minsky, H. P. 1959: A linear model of cyclical growth. *Review of Economics and Statistics*, 41(2), 133–45.

Minsky, H. P. 1977: A theory of systematic financial instability. In E. I. Altman and A. W. Sametz (eds), *Financial Crises, Institutions and Markets in a Fragile Environment*. New York: John Wiley, 138–52.

Minsky, H. P. 1982a: *Can 'IT' Happen Again? Essays on Instability in Finance*. New York: M. E. Sharpe.

Minsky, H. P. 1982b: The financial instability hypothesis: capitalist process and the behaviour of the economy. In C. P. Kindleberger and J. P. Laffargue (eds), *Financial Crises: Theory, History and Policy*. Cambridge: Cambridge University Press, ch. 2.

Minsky, H. P. 1986: *Stabilising an Unstable Economy*. New Haven: Yale University Press.

Mirowski, P. 1990: From Mandelbrot to chaos. *Economic Journal*, 57(2), 289–307.

Mishkin, P. S. 1981: The real interest rate: an empirical investigation. *Carnegie–Rochester Conference Series on Public Policy*, 15, 151–200.

Mishkin, P. S. 1982: Does anticipated money matter? An econometric investigation. *Journal of Political Economy*, 90, 22–51.

Modigliani, F. 1944: Liquidity preference and the theory of interest and money. *Econometrica*, 12, 45–88.

Muellbauer, J. and Portes, R. 1978: Macroeconomic models with quantity rationing. *Economic Journal*, 88, 788–821.

Mullineux, A. W. 1984: *The Business Cycle After Keynes: a Contemporary Analysis*. Hemel Hempstead: Harvester Wheatsheaf/Totowa, New Jersey: Barnes and Noble.

Mullineux, A. W. 1990: *Business Cycles and Financial Crises*. Hemel Hempstead: Harvester Wheatsheaf/Ann Arbor: University of Michigan Press.

Mullineux, A. W. and Dickinson, D. G. 1992: Real business cycles: theory and evidence. *Journal of Economic Surveys*, 6(4), 321–58.

Mullineux, A. W. and Peng, W. 1993: Nonlinear business cycle modelling. *Journal of Economic Surveys*, 7(1), 41–83.

Murphy, K. M. and Topel, R. H. 1987: The evolution of unemployment in the United States: 1968–85. *Macroeconomics Annual*, National Bureau of Economic Research.

Neftci, S. N. 1984: Are economic time series asymmetric over the business cycle? *Journal of Political Economy*, 92, 307–28.

Neftci, S. N. 1986: Is there a cyclical time unit? In K. Brunner and A. H. Meltzer (ed.), *The National Bureau Method, International Capital Mobility and Other Essays*. Carnegie–Rochester Conference Series on Public Policy 24. Amsterdam: North Holland, 11–48.

Neftci, S. N. and McNevin, B. 1986: Some evidence on the non-linearity of economic time series: 1892–1981. C. V. Starr Center for Applied Economics, New York University, New York.

Nelson, C. R. and Plosser, C. I. 1982: Trends and random walks in macroeconomic time series. *Journal of Monetary Economics*, 10, 139–62.

Nordhaus, W. D. 1975: The political business cycle. *Review of Economic Studies*, 42, 169–90.

Nordhaus, W. D. 1989: Alternative approaches to the political business cycle. *Brookings Papers on Economic Activity*, no. 2, 1–68.

Norrbin, S. C. and Schlagenhauf, D. E. 1988: An inquiry into the sources of macroeconomic fluctuations. *Journal of Monetary Economics*, 22, 43–70.

Nusse, H. E. and Hommes, C. H. 1990: Resolutions of chaos with application to a modified Samuelson model. *Journal of Economic Dynamics and Control*, 14, 1–19.

Okun, A. M. 1980: Rational expectations with misperceptions as a theory of the business cycle. *Journal of Money, Credit and Banking*, 12, 817–25.

Otto, G. and Wirjanto, T. 1990: Seasonal unit-root tests on Canadian macroeconomic time series. *Economics Letters*, 34, 117–20.

Parkin, M. 1986: The output–inflation trade-off when prices are costly to change. *Journal of Political Economy*, 94, 200–24.

Pauls, B. D. 1987: Comovements in aggregate and relative prices. *Journal of Monetary Economics*, 20, 155–68.

Peltzeman, S. 1990: How efficient is the voting market? *Journal of Law and Economics*, XXXIII (April), 27–63.

Peng, W. S. 1991: Chaos, nonlinearity and monetary aggregates, Department of Economics, University of Birmingham (UK), discussion paper no. 91–02.

Perron, P. 1989: The great crash, the oil price shock and the unit root hypothesis. *Econometrica*, 56, 1361–401.

Perron, P. and Phillips, P. C. B. 1987: Does GNP have a unit root? *Economics Letters*, 23, 139–45.

Persson, M. 1979: Rational expectations in log linear models. *Scandinavian Journal of Economics*, 81, 378–86.

Pissarides, C. A. 1972: A model of British macroeconomic policy, 1955–1969. *Manchester School*, 40, 245–59.

Pohjolu, M. T. 1979: Wages, prices and the stability of the class struggle. Faculty of Economics and Politics, University of Cambridge, research paper no. 12.

Pohjolu, M. T. 1981: Stable cyclic and chaotic growth: the dynamics of a discrete time version of Goodwin's growth cycle model. *Zeitschrift für Nationalökonomie*, 41, 27–38.

Prescott, E. C. 1986: Theory ahead of business cycle measurement. In K. Brunner and A. H. Meltzer (eds), *Real Business Cycles, Real Exchange Rates and Actual Policies*. Carnegie–Rochester Conference Series on Public Policy 25. Amsterdam: North Holland, 11–24.

Puu, T. 1986: Multiplier–accelerator models revisited. *Regional Science and Urban Economics*, 16(1), 81–95.

Ramsey, J. B. and Yuan, H. 1989a: Bias and error bars in dimension calculations and their evaluation on some simple models. *Physics Letters A*, 134, 187–97.

Ramsey, J. B. and Yuan, H. 1989b: The statistical properties of dimension calculation using small data sets. *Nonlinearity*, 2, 253–64.

Ramsey, J. B., Sayers, C. L. and Rothman, P. 1990: The statistical properties of dimension calculations using small data sets: some economic applications. *International Economic Review*, 3(4), 991–1020.

Rau, N. 1974: *Trade Cycles: Theories and Evidence*. London: Macmillan.

Reichlin, P. 1986: Equilibrium cycles in an overlapping generations economy with production. *Journal of Economic Theory*, 40, 89–102.

Rogerson, R. 1987: An equilibrium model of sectoral allocation. *Journal of Political Economy*, 95, 824–34.

Rogerson, R. 1988: Indivisible labour, lotteries and equilibrium. *Journal of Monetary Economics*, 21, 3–16.

Rogerson, R. and Rupert, P. 1991: New estimates of intertemporal substitution, *Journal of Monetary Economics*, 27, 255–69.

Rogoff, K. 1987: Reputational constraints on monetary policy. In K. Brunner and A. H. Meltzer (eds), *Bubbles and Other Essays*. Carnegie–Rochester Conference Series on Public Policy 26. Amsterdam: North Holland, 148–82.

Rogoff, K. 1989: Reputation, coordination and monetary policy. In R. J. Barro (ed.), *Handbook of Modern Business Cycle Theory*. Cambridge, Massachusetts: Harvard University Press.

Rogoff, K. 1990: Equilibrium political budget cycles. *American Economic Review*, 80(1), 21–36.

Rogoff, K. and Sibert, A. 1988: Equilibrium political business cycles. *Review of Economic Studies*, 55 (January), 1–16.

Romer, C. D. 1991: The cyclical behaviour of individual production series, 1889–1984. *Quarterly Journal of Economics*, 106, 1–31.

Romer, P. M. 1986: Increasing returns, specialization, and external economics: growth as described by Allyn Young. Center for Economic Research, University of Rochester, Rochester, New York, working paper no. 64.

Romer, P. M. 1989: Capital accumulation in the theory of long-run growth. In R. J. Barro (ed.), *Modern Business Cycle Theory*. Cambridge, Massachusetts: Harvard University Press.

Romer, P. M. 1990: Endogenous technical change. *Journal of Political Economy*, 98(2), 71–102.

Rose, H. 1967: On the nonlinear theory of the employment cycle. *Review of Economic Studies*, 34, 138–52.

Rose, H. 1969: Real and monetary factors in the business cycle. *Journal of Money, Credit and Banking*, May, 138–52.

Rotemberg, J. J. 1986: Is there a cyclical time unit? A comment. In K. Brunner and A. H. Meltzer (eds), *The National Bureau Method, International Capital Mobility and Other Essays*. Carnegie–Rochester Conference Series on Public Policy 24. Amsterdam: North Holland, 49–53.

Rotemberg, J. J. and Summers, L. H. 1990: Inflexible prices and pro-cyclical productivity. *Quarterly Journal of Economics*, 105, 857–74.

Roubini, N. and Sachs, J. 1989: Political and economic determinants of budget deficits in the industrial democracies. *European Economic Review*, 33, 903–33.

Samuelson, P. A. 1939: Interaction between the multiplier analysis and the acceleration principle. *Review of Economics and Statistics*, 31, 75–8.

Samuelson, P. A. 1947: *Foundations of Economic Analysis*. Cambridge, Massachusetts: Harvard University Press.

Samuelson, P. A. 1965: A theory of induced innovations along Kennedy–Weizacker lines. *Review of Economics and Statistics*, 47(4), 343–56.

Samuelson, P. A. 1967: A universal cycle? *Operations Research Vefahren*, 3, 307–20.

Samuelson, P. A. 1971: Generalized predator-prey oscillations in ecological and economic equilibrium. *Proceedings of the National Academy of Sciences*, USA, 68, 487–90.

Sargent, T. J. 1976: The observational equivalence of natural and unnatural rate theories of macroeconomies. *Journal of Political Economy*, 84, 631–40.

Sargent, T. J. 1987: *Macroeconomic Theory*, 2nd edn. New York: Academic Press.

Sargent, T. J. and Wallace, N. 1975: Rational expectations, the optimal monetary instrument and the optimal money supply rule. *Journal of Political Economy*, 53(2), 241–54.

Sargent, T. J. and Wallace, N. 1976: Rational expectations and the theory of economic policy. *Journal of Monetary Economics*, 2(2), 169–83.

Savin, N. E. 1977: A test of the Monte-Carlo hypothesis: comment. *Economic Inquiry*, 15, 613–17.

Sayers, C. 1986: Work stoppages: exploring the nonlinear dynamics. Mimeo. Department of Economics, University of Wisconsin, Madison, Wisconsin.

Sayers, C. 1987: Diagnostic tests for nonlinearity in time series data: an application to the work stoppings series. Mimeo, Department of Economics, University of Houston.

Sayers, C. 1990: Chaos and the business cycle. In S. Krasner (ed.), *The Ubiquity of Chaos*. New York: American Association for the Advance of Science, 115–25.

Scheinkman, J. A. 1984: General equilibrium models of economic fluctuations: a survey of theory. Chicago, University of Chicago working paper.

Scheinkman, J. A. 1990: Nonlinearities in economic dynamics. *Economic Journal*, 100 (Suppl.), 33–48.

Scheinkman, J. A. and LeBaron, B. 1987: Nonlinear dynamics and GNP data. Department of Economics, University of Chicago.

Scheinkman, J. A. and LeBaron, B. 1989: Nonlinear dynamics and stock returns. *Journal of Business*, July, 311–37.

Scheinkman, J. A. and Weiss, L. 1986: Borrowing constraints and aggregate economic activity. *Econometrica*, 54, 23–45.

Schinasi, G. J. 1981: A nonlinear dynamic model of short run fluctuations. *Review of Economic Studies*, 48(4), 649–56.

Schinasi, G. J. 1982: Fluctuations in a dynamic, intermediate-run IS–LM model: applications of the Poincaré–Bendixon theorem. *Journal of Economic Theory*, 28, 369–75.

Schlagenhauf, D. E. and Wrase, J. 1991: Liquidity and real activity in a simple open economy model. Working paper, Arizona State University.

Schumpeter, J. A. 1934: *Theory of Economic Development*. Oxford: Oxford University Press. (reprinted 1967).

Schumpeter, J. A. 1935: The analysis of economic change. *Review of Economics and Statistics*, 17, 2–10.

Schumpeter, J. A. 1939: *Business Cycles: a Theoretical, Historical and Statistical Analysis of the Capitalist Process*, 2 vols. New York: McGraw-Hill, reprinted in abridged form 1964.

Schwert, G. W. 1987: Effect of model specification on tests for unit roots in macroeconomic data. *Journal of Monetary Economics*, 20, 73–103.

Schwert, G. W. 1989: Tests of unit roots: a Monte Carlo investigation. *Journal of Business and Economics Statistics*, 7, 147–59.

Sen, P. K. 1972: Limited behaviour of regular functionals of empirical distributions for stationary process. *Zeitschrift für Wahrscheinlichkeitstheorie und Verwandte Gebiete*, 25, 71–82.

Serfling, R. 1980: *Approximation Theorems of Mathematical Statistics*. New York: John Wiley.

Shackle, G. L. S. 1968: *Expectations, Investment and Income*, lst edn 1938. Oxford: Oxford University Press.

Shapiro, M. D. and Watson, M. W. 1988: Sources of business cycle fluctuations. *Macroeconomics Annual, National Bureau of Economic Research*, 111–48.

Sharpe, W. F. 1964: Capital asset prices: a theory of market equilibrium under conditional risk. *Journal of Finance*, 19, 425–42.

Shell, K. 1977: Monnaie et allocation intertemporelle. Mimeo. Paris: INSEE.

Sichel, D. E. 1989: Are business cycles asymmetric? A correction. *Journal of Political Economy*, 97, 1255–60.

Sims, C. A. 1980: Comparison of interwar and postwar cycles: monetarism reconsidered. *American Economic Review*, 70, 250–7.

Sims, C. A. 1982: Policy analysis and econometric models. *Brookings Papers on Economic Activity*, 1, 107–52.

Sims, C. A. 1986: Comments. In H. F. Sonnerschein (ed.), *Models of Economic Dynamics*. New York: Springer-Verlag.

Sinai, A. 1978: Credit crunch possibility and the crunch barometer. *Data Resources Review*, June, 9–18.

Sinai, A. 1980: Crunch impacts and the aftermath. *Data Resources Review*, June, 37–60.

Singleton, K. J. 1987: Speculation and the volatility of foreign currency exchange rates. In K. Brunner and A. H. Meltzer (eds), *Bubbles and Other Essays*. Carnegie–Rochester Conference Series 26. Amsterdam: North Holland, 9–56.

Singleton, K. J. 1988: Econometric issues in the analysis of equilibrium business cycle models. *Journal of Monetary Economics*, 21, 361–86.

Slutsky, E. 1937: The summation of random causes as the source of cyclical processes. *Econometrica*, 5, 105–46.

Smith, B. D. 1989a: Unemployment, the variability of hours, and the persistence of disturbances: a private information approach. *International Economic Review*, 30, 921–938.

Smith, B. D. 1989b: A business cycle model with private information. *Journal of Labour Economics*, 7, 210–237.

Smith, J. and Murphy, C. 1991: Macroeconomic fluctuations in the Australian economy. Working papers in Economics and Econometrics no. 222. The Australian National University.

Smithies, A. 1957: Economic fluctuations and growth. *Econometrica*, 25(1), 1–52.

Solomou, S. 1987: *Phases of Economic Growth 1850–1973: Kondratieff Waves and Kuznets Swings*. Cambridge: Cambridge University Press.

Solow, R. 1956: A contribution to the theory of economic growth. *Quarterly Journal of Economics*, 70, 65–94.

Solow, R. M. 1957: Technical change and the aggregate production function. *Review of Economic and Statistics*, 39, 312–20.

Solow, R. 1970: *Growth Theory*. New York: Oxford University Press.

Sparrow, C. 1982: *The Lorenz Equations*. New York and Berlin: Springer-Verlag.

Stadler, G. W. 1990: Business cycle models with endogenous technology. *American Economic Review*, 80, 763–78.

Stiglitz, J. E. and Weiss, A. 1981: Credit rationing in markets with imperfect information. *American Economic Review*, 71, 393–410.

Stock, J. H. and Watson, M. W. 1988: Testing for common trends. *Journal of the American Statistical Association*, 83, 1097–107.

Stockman, A. C. 1988: Real business cycle theory: a guide, and evaluation, and new direction. *Economic Review* (Federal Reserve Bank of Cleveland), 24, 24–47.

Stockman, A. C. 1990: International transmission and real business cycle models. *American Economic Review*, 80, 134–8.

Stultz, R. 1986: Interest rates and monetary policy uncertainty. *Journal of Monetary Economics*, 17, 331–47.

Stutzer, M. J. 1980: Chaotic dynamics and bifurcation in a macro model. *Journal of Economic Dynamics and Control*, 2, 353–76.

Subba Rao, T. and Gabr, M. 1980: A test for linearity of stationary time series. *Journal of Time Series Analysis*, 1, 145–58.

Subba Rao, T. and Gabr, M. 1984: *An Introduction to Bispectral Analysis and Bilinear Time Series Models*. Lecture Notes in Statistics 24. New York: Springer–Verlag.

Svensson, L. E. O. 1985: Money and asset prices in a cash-in-advance economy. *Journal of Political Economy*, 33, 919–44.

Svensson, L. E. O. 1989: Portfolio choice with non-expected utility in continuous time. *Economics Letters*, 30, 313–17.

Takens, F. 1983: Distinguishing deterministic and random systems. In G. Borenblatt, G. Iooss, and D. Joseph (eds), *Nonlinear Dynamics and Turbulence*. Boston: Pitman.

Taylor, J. B. 1979: Staggered wage setting in a macro world. *American Economic Review*, 69 (papers and proceedings), 109–13.

Thom, R. 1975: *Structural Stability and Morphogenesis*. New York: Benjamin.

Tufte, E. R. 1978: *Political Control of the Economy*. Princeton, New Jersey: Princeton University Press.

Tullock, G. 1976: The vote motive. Hobart Paper 9. London: Institute of Economic Affairs.

Turner, P. M. 1991: A structural vector autoregression model of the UK business cycle. University of Leeds, August.

Van der Ploeg, F. 1984: Implications of workers' savings for economic growth and class struggle. In Goodwin et al. (1984) op. cit., 1–13.

Van der Ploeg, F. 1986: Rational expectations, risk and chaos in financial markets. *Economic Journal*, 96 (Suppl.), 151–62.

Varian, H. 1979: Catastrophe theory and the business cycle. *Economic Inquiry*, 17, 14–28.

Velupillai, K. 1979: Some stability properties of Goodwin's growth cycle. *Zeitschrift für Nationalökonomie*, 39, 245–57.

Volterra, V. 1926: Fluctuations in the abundance of species considered mathematically. *Nature*, CXVIII, 558–60.

Walton, D. R. 1988: Does GNP have a unit root? Evidence for the UK. *Economics Letters*, 26(3), 219–24.

Watson, M. W. 1986: Univariate detrending methods with stochastic trends. *Journal of Monetary Economics*, 18(1), 49–76.

Weil, P. 1990: Non-expected utility in macroeconomics. *Quarterly Journal of Economics*, 106, 29–42.

Weiss, L. 1984: Asymmetric adjustment costs and sectoral shifts. Department of Economics, University of California, San Diego.

West, K. D. 1987: A standard monetary model and the variability of the Deutschemark–dollar exchange rate. *Journal of International Economics*, 23, 57–76.

West, K. D. 1990: Sources of cycles in Japan, 1975–1987. Working paper, University of Wisconsin, Madison, Wisconsin.

West, K. D. 1991: Sources of cycles in Japan, 1975–1987. *Journal of Japanese and International Economics.*

Whiteley, P. (ed.) 1980: *Models of Political Economy.* London: Sage.

Willett, T. D. (ed.) 1984: *Political Business Cycles.* Durham, North Carolina: Duke University Press.

Williamson, S. D. 1987: Financial intermediation, business failures and real business cycles. *Journal of Political Economy,* 95, 1196–216.

Wolf, A., Swift, J., Swinney, H. and Vastano, J. 1985: Determining Lyapunov exponents from a time series. *Physica D,* 16, 285–317.

Woodford, M. 1988a: Expectation, finance constraints and aggregate in stability. In M. Kohn and S. C. Tsiang (eds), *Finance Constraints, Expectations and Macroeconomics.* New York: Oxford University Press.

Woodford, M. 1988b: Imperfect financial intermediation and complex dynamics. In W. Barnett, J. Geweke and K. Shell (eds), *Economic Complexity: Chaos, Sunspots, Bubbles and Nonlinearity.* Cambridge: Cambridge University Press.

Woodford, M. 1990: Learning to believe in sunspots. *Econometrica,* 58(2), 277–307.

Zarnowitz, V. 1985: Recent work on business cycles in historical perspective. *Journal of Economic Literature,* 23(2), 523–80.

Zeeman, C. 1977: *Catastrophe Theory: Selected Papers 1972–1977.* Reading Massachusetts: Addison-Wesley.

Index

Abraham, K. G., 19
acceleration principle, 3
adaptive expectations, 66, 75, 76
Adelman, I., 31
Akerlof, G. A., 129
Akerman, J., 64–5
Alesina, A., 64, 74–6, 79, 81, 82, 104, 106, 107
Alt, J. E., 79
Amendola, M., 127
ARIMA specification, 22
Attfield, C. L. P., 16
Australia, 94
Austria, 23
autocovariance analysis, 59
Azariadis, C., 48–9, 127, 129

Backus, D. K., 71, 73, 75
Balducci, R., 43
Balke, N. S., 22, 75–6
banks and banking, 43, 126–7
    central, 76, 77, 80–1
Barnett, W. A., 55, 58, 60
Barro, R. J., 2, 3, 12, 15, 16, 18, 67, 69–71, 74
Baumol, W. J., 33, 45
BDS test, 59, 116–18
Beck, N., 80
Begg, D. K. H., 51
Bencivenga, V. R., 11, 127
Benhabib, J., 33, 45, 47, 49–50, 53
Bewley, T., 47, 50
bifurcations, 32, 127

bispectrum tests, 59–60
Black, P., 8, 17
Blanchard, O. J., 20, 21, 92, 93, 94, 126, 127
Blatt, J. M., 26–7, 33, 53, 61
Boddy, R., 1, 65
Boldrin, M., 26, 45, 46–7, 50, 51, 124
Brock, W. A., 21, 33, 54, 55, 57, 58, 59, 60, 61, 110, 113
Bronfenbrenner, M., 1
budget cycles, 73, 76, 81, 82, 105, 109
Bufman, G., 129
Butler, A., 45

Campbell, J. Y., 22, 88, 127
Canada, 58
Cantor, R., 14
Canzoneri, M. O., 72–3
cash-in-advance constraint, 12, 51, 128
catastrophe theory, 39, 44–5
central banks, 76, 77, 80–1
Chan, L. K. C., 16
Chang, W. W., 39
chaos theory, 21, 25–6, 27, 33–4
    business cycle models in, 45–53
    empirical evidence of, 53–8, 110–13, 119
Chappell, H. W., 80
Chappell, D., 81
Chen, P., 27, 55, 58
Chiarella, C., 43–4

Christiano, L. J., 20
Chrystal, K. A., 21, 79
Clarke, P. K., 22
class-conflict model, 41–2
Cochrane, J. H., 22, 23
cointegration concept, 23, 91–2
conservative cycles, 31
Cooper, R., 15
corner solutions, 19
correlation dimension, 55–6, 110,
    112–13
credibility, 65, 67–74, 122–3
credit crunches, 126
credit rationing, 11
Crotty, J., 1, 65
Cuckierman, A., 72, 75
Cugno, F., 51
cusp catastrophe, 44–5

Davis, S. J., 19
Day, R. H., 40, 46, 47, 49–50, 51–2
De Long, J. B., 61
Desai, M., 40, 41
Dickey–Fuller test, 21, 89, 92, 95
Dickinson, D. G., 47
Di Matteo, M., 42–3
discontinuities, 32
Dotsey, M., 15
Dowd, K., 21
Downs, A., 1, 66
Driffill, J., 71, 73, 75
Duesenberry, J., 35
Durlauf, S. N., 21
DYMIMIC approach, 21
dynamic economic development,
    28, 41
dynamic time series, 21

Eckstein, A., 126
Eichenbaum, M., 11–12, 18, 20
electoral economic cycle, 65,
    66–7, 79, 81–2
Ellis, C. J., 75, 76
endogenous fluctuations, non-
    linear models with, 45–53

endogenous growth model, 10,
    18, 125
Engle, R. P., 21, 60, 91–2
equilibrium business cycle, 1–4,
    23–4, 120, 122
  basic model of, 5–9
  empirical evidence of, 15–23,
    121
  extensions of, 9–15
  future research suggestions in,
    125–6
  non-linear, 27, 28, 32, 45–53, 62
  see also real equilibrium
    business cycles
European Monetary System, 123
evolutionary economics, 28
exchange rates, 95, 99
expectations
  adaptive, 66, 75, 76
  rational, 1, 3, 43, 47, 126, 128
    political business cycles and,
    65, 66–7, 68, 73, 76, 83, 84,
    101, 105

Feiwel, G. R., 65
financial intermediation, 11
financial sector *see* banks and
    banking
fiscal policy, 15, 80–1, 108–9
Fisher, I., 2, 46
Flacco, P. R., 127
Flood, R. P., 126
fold catastrophe, 44
Fomby, T. B., 22
Ford, J. L., 28
Frank, M. Z., 26, 45, 58
Frey, B. S., 1, 74–5, 76, 77, 83
Friedlaender, A. F., 78
Friedman, M., 9, 12, 91
Frisch, R., 3, 5, 25, 31
future research, suggestions for,
    123–9

Gabisch, G., 51
Gabr, M., 59

Gaffard, J.-L., 127
game theory, 14, 43
  political business cycles and,
    67–74, 125
Garber, P. M., 12, 126
Gaynon, J. E., 90
George, D. A. R., 26, 43
Germany, 123
Glombowski, J., 43
Goodwin, R. M., 36, 39, 40,
  41–3, 45, 51
Gordon, D. B., 69–71, 74
Gordon, R. J., 2, 3, 16, 64, 67
Grandmont, J. M., 47–8, 50, 124
Granger, C. W. J., 87, 91–2
Grassberger, P., 55–6, 112
Greenwald, B., 25, 129
Greenwood, J., 15
Grier, K. B., 80–1
Grinols, E. L., 127, 128
Grossman, S. J., 13
growth theory/models, 35, 41–2,
  125
  neoclassical, 8–10, 17–18, 27–8,
    128
  non-linear, 46–7
Guesnerie, R., 48–9

Haberler, G., 2
Hall, R. E., 91
Haltiwanger, J. L., 15
Hansen, A. H., 2
Hansen, G., 19
Harrod, R. F., 35
Harvey, A. C., 87
Havrilinsky, T. M., 76
Hayek, F. von, 1
Haynes, S. E., 82–3
Hercowitz, Z., 16
Herzel, H., 55
heterogeneous agents, 15
Hibbs, D. A., 67, 75, 77, 79, 80,
  81
Hickman, B. G., 31
Hicks, J. R., 27, 32, 35, 36, 39

Hinich, M., 59, 60
Hommes, C. H., 51
Hotelling, H., 66
Huffman, G. N., 15
Hylleberg, S., 22

Ichimura, S., 36, 39
induced investment, 36
inflation, 39
  political business cycles and,
    66–84 *passim*, 105
input–output relationships, 8
interest rates, 14–15, 20, 43, 48,
  52, 128
international transmission of
    business cycles, 14
intertemporal substitution, 7–8,
  9, 23
inventories, 15
investment and saving, 14, 36, 38
islands hypothesis, 8

Jevons, W. S., 49

Kaldor, N., 36–9, 40, 42, 44
Kalecki, M., 1, 64, 65
Katz, L. P., 19
Keech, W. R., 80
Keil, M. W., 82, 83
Kelsey, D., 26, 33, 45, 46, 50
Keynes, J. M., 12, 49
Keynesianism, 2, 3
  non-linear business cycle
    model in, 27, 35–41, 52
Kim, K., 22
Kindleberger, C. P., 49, 126
King, R. G., 9–11, 12, 15, 17–18,
  23, 27, 125, 128
Klein, L. R., 31, 39, 52
Kondratief waves, 50
Kosobud, R. F., 39, 52
Kreps, D., 128
Kretzmer, P. E., 16
Krol, R., 20
Kruger, M., 43

Kunst, R., 23
Kurths, J., 55
Kydland, F. E., 6, 8–9, 10, 11, 12, 15, 16–17, 19, 26, 53, 68, 69, 74, 128

labour market, 9, 19, 23, 41
Lachler, U., 81
large infrequent hypothesis, 22
Laroque, G., 50
learning process, 50
LeBaron, B., 57, 58, 60
Leiderman, L., 129
Leijonhufvud, A., 45
Lillien, D. M., 19
limit cycles, 32–3, 39
Lin, T. Y., 40, 51–2
Lindbeck, A., 64
Lines, M., 3
Litterman, R. B., 20
Ljungqvist, L., 20
Long, J. B., 6, 7–8, 19, 21, 53
Lorenz, H. W., 39, 41, 51
Lucas, R. E., 1–2, 3, 5, 10, 11, 12–14, 16, 51, 67, 68, 128
Luckett, D. G., 80
Lyapunov exponents, 55, 110

McCallum, B. T., 20, 67, 79, 81, 103
Maccini, L. J., 15
MacRae, D., 64, 66, 67
Magill, M. S. P., 47
Malliaris, A. G., 23
Mankiw, N., 18, 22, 88, 127
Mark, N. C., 14
market failure, 129
Marx, K., 41, 42
Mathews, R. C. O., 32
May, A. M., 77
median voter theorem, 66
Meltzer, A. H., 73, 75
Mendoza, E. G., 14, 17
Merrick, J. J., 16
Metcalfe, J. S., 50

Mezler, L. A., 40
Mills, T., 22, 91
Minford, P., 67
Minsky, H. P., 126, 127
Mishkin, P. S., 16
modern political economists, 1
Modigliani, F., 40
monetary equilibrium business cycles (MBC), 2, 3, 5–6, 8, 12–13, 120
money and money supply, 94–5, 96, 98
  in non-linear business cycle models, 40, 42–3, 47–8, 52
  in political business cycles, 76, 80, 105–7
  in real equilibrium business cycles, 10–11, 12–13, 16, 19–20, 23, 126–7
Monte Carlo hypothesis, 2, 46
Montrucchio, L., 51
Mullineux, A. W., 1, 2, 3, 43, 45, 61, 65, 66, 77, 78, 126
multipliers, 18, 28, 35
Murphy, C., 94

National Bureau of Economic Research, 2, 26
Neftci, S. N., 53, 60–1
Nelson, C. R., 21, 23, 57, 86, 87
neoclassical growth theory, 8–10, 17–18, 27–8, 128
Neusser, K., 23
new classical school, 2, 47, 67
New Keynesianism, 11, 19, 25, 48, 127, 129
Newbold, P., 87
Nishimura, K., 47, 53
non-expected utility, 128–9
non-linear business cycle models, 25–8, 61–3, 120–1
  compared with linear models, 28–34
  empirical evidence of, 53–61, 109–18, 119

endogenous fluctuations and
   chaos in, 45–53
future research suggestions for,
   123–4
Keynesian, 27, 35–41, 52
miscellaneous, 41–5
non-linear growth models
   (NGMs), 46–7
non-market clearing, 129
non-stationarity, empirical
   evidence of, 85–92
Nordhaus, W. D., 1, 64, 65, 66,
   67–8, 73, 77, 80, 81, 100, 105
Norrbin, S. C., 21
Nusse, H. E., 51

Ohonian, L. E., 20
Okun, A. M., 3
O'Neill, W. D., 39, 52
open economy models, 14–15,
   17, 92
Otto, G., 22
output tax, 15
overlapping generations models
   (OGMs), 46, 47–51
Oxley, L. T., 26, 43

Parker, R. E., 127
Parkin, M., 129
partisanship, 65, 74–7, 79–80, 82–3
Patterson, D. M., 59
Peel, D., 67, 81
Peltzeman, S., 66
Peng, W. S., 28, 43, 45, 60
permanent income hypothesis,
   91–2
Perron, P., 21–2
persistent hypothesis, 22, 85–92,
   124
Persson, M., 47
Phillips, P. C. B., 21–2
Phillips curve, 39–40, 68–71, 76
Pissarides, C. A., 78
Plosser, C. I., 6, 7–8, 10–11, 19,
   21, 23, 53, 57, 86, 87

Pohjolu, M. T., 51
policy convergence, 66
policy implications of business
   cycles, 122–3
political budget cycles, 73, 76, 81,
   82, 105, 109
political business cycles, 1, 2,
   64–5, 84, 121
   electoral economic cycle
      approach to, 65, 66–7, 79,
      81–2
   empirical evidence of, 77–83,
      100–9, 119
   future research suggestions for,
      125–6
   partisanship and, 65, 74–7,
      79–80, 82–3
   reputation and credibility in,
      65, 67–74, 122–3
Porteus, E., 128
Potts, G. T., 80
Prescott, E. C., 6, 8–9, 10, 11, 12,
   15, 16–17, 18, 19, 26, 53, 68,
   69, 74, 128
Preston, R. S., 31, 39, 52
Procaccia, I., 55–6, 112
production possibility hypothesis, 8
productivity shocks, 7, 9, 16–17,
   18, 23, 96, 125
Puu, T., 51

Quah, D., 92

Ramsey, J. B., 27, 54, 57, 58, 60
rational expectations, 1, 3, 43, 47,
   126, 128
   political business cycles and,
      65, 66–7, 68, 73, 76, 83, 84,
      101, 105
rational ignorance hypothesis, 66,
   67
real equilibrium business cycles, 2,
   3–4, 23–4, 25, 27–8, 31, 120
   basic model of, 5–9
   empirical evidence of, 15–23, 26

extensions of, 9–15
future research suggestions for, 125, 126, 128–9
Rebelo, S. T., 18, 128
Reichlin, P., 51
reputation, 65, 67–74, 122–3
research suggestions, 123–9
residual tests, 57, 110–13
risk and uncertainty, 72–3, 123, 127–9
Rogerson, R., 19
Rogoff, K., 71, 73, 75, 76, 81, 105, 109
Romer, P. M., 10, 125
Rose, H., 39–40
Roubini, N., 104, 108

Sachs, J., 82, 108
Samuelson, P. A., 3, 26, 28, 31, 32, 40, 41, 51
Sargent, T. J., 2, 13–14, 67, 150,
saving and investment, 14, 36, 38
Sayers, C. L., 21, 33, 58, 60, 61, 110
Scheinkman, J. A., 11, 13, 45, 46, 57, 58, 60
Schinasi, G. J., 39
Schlagenhauf, D. E., 21
Schmidt, P., 22
Schneider, F., 74, 76, 77, 83
Schumpeter, J. A., 28, 41, 42, 127
Schwartz, A. J., 12
Schwert, G. W., 21, 22
search theory, 19
seasonal factors, 22
self-fulfilling prophecies, 49
Sen, P. K., 59
Serfling, R., 59
Shackle, G. L. S., 28, 41, 127
Shafer, J. W., 40, 51–2
Shah, A., 41
Shapiro, M. D., 20–1
Shell, K., 48
shock-generation model, 3, 124
shuffle diagnostic, 57

Sibert, A., 73, 105, 109
signal extraction problem, 6, 9, 13
Sims, C. A., 20, 50, 51, 92, 93
Sinai, A., 126
Singleton, K. J., 11–12, 20, 124
Slutsky, E., 3, 31
small frequent hypothesis, 22
Smith, B. D., 11, 15, 127
Smith, J., 94
Smithies, A., 35
Smyth, D. J., 39
Solomou, S., 50
Solow, R. M., 18, 46
spectral analysis, 59
speculation, 49, 126
Stengos, T., 26, 45, 48
Stiglitz, J. E., 11, 25, 129
Stock, J. H., 20, 88
Stockman, A. C., 14
Stokey, N. L., 12, 13, 51
Stone, J. A., 82–3
Stultz, R., 128
Stutzer, M. J., 51
Subba Rao, T., 59
Summers, L. H., 61
sunspot equilibria, 46, 48–9
surprise supply function, 16
Svensson, L. E. O., 128, 129

Takens, F., 54
taxation *see* fiscal policy
Taylor, J. B., 13, 129
Taylor, M. P., 22
technology shocks, 9, 10, 14, 28, 124, 126–7
Thom, R., 64
time-inconsistency, 68, 69, 102
trade, international, 14
Tufte, E. R., 1, 80, 82
Tullock, G., 1
Turner, P. M., 92, 94, 95, 98
Turnovsky, S. J., 127, 128

ultra-rationality hypothesis, 77, 80
uncertainty, 72–3, 123, 127–9

unit root tests, 21–2, 89–90, 95, 121
United Kingdom, 85–92, 118–19
  chaos and non-linearity in, 60,
    109–18, 119
  equilibrium business cycles in,
    21, 22
  policy implications for, 122–3
  political business cycles in, 79,
    82, 100–9, 119
  VAR model of, 92–9, 119, 121
United States of America
  equilibrium business cycles in,
    16
  non-linearity and chaos in, 58,
    60, 61
  political business cycles in, 76,
    79–81, 82–3
Urrutia, J. L., 23
U-statistic theory, 59

Van der Ploeg, F., 42, 51
variable utilization of capital, 15,
    17

Varian, H., 39, 44–5
vector autoregressions (VARs),
    20, 92–9, 119, 121
Volterra–Lotka equations, 41

Wallace, N., 2, 67
Wlaton, D. R., 22, 86
Watson, M. W., 20–1, 22, 88,
    126
Weil, P., 129
Weiss, A., 11
Weiss, L., 11, 13, 20
West, K. D., 95
Williamson, S. D., 11
Wirjanto, T., 22
Wolf, A., 55
Woodford, M., 26, 45, 46–7, 49,
    50, 51, 124

Yellen, J. L., 129
Yuan, H., 58

Zarnowitz, V., 8, 63

9 780631 185673